Houseplants

Houseplants

Plants to add style and glamour to your home

NEW
HOLLAND

First published in 2012 by New Holland Publishers (UK) Ltd
London • Cape Town • Sydney • Auckland

Garfield House, 86–88 Edgware Rd, London, W2 2EA, United Kingdom
80 McKenzie Street, Cape Town, 8001, South Africa
Unit 1, 66 Gibbes Street, Chatswood NSW 2067, Australia
218 Lake Road, Northcote, Auckland, New Zealand

ISBN 978 184773 859 2

Publisher: Clare Sayer
Editor: Marilyn Inglis
Designer: Geoff Borin (www.geoffborin.com)
Production: Laurence Poos
Photography: Clive Nichols

10 9 8 7 6 5 4 3 2 1

Reproduction by Pica Digital PTE Ltd, Singapore
Printed and bound in China by Toppan Leefung Printing Ltd

Contents

Introduction

ABOVE *Even a small unassuming houseplant will add a welcome extra dimension to an interior.*

OPPOSITE PAGE *Sun-loving* Aeonium arboreum *'Schwarzkopf' and bronze Air plants (top left) are perfectly complemented by sun-baked terracotta and driftwood. The Glory lily (*Gloriosa superba *'Rothschildiana' top right) is brilliantly colourful but its flowers are exquisitely shaped. With all the uplifting promise of spring, just a few hyacinths (bottom left) will fill a room with their sweet, heady fragrance. Given the space, indoor plants can be productive as well as decorative (bottom right); here melons and tomatoes scramble up rustic obelisks and onto the conservatory wall beyond.*

I have been growing houseplants for as long as I can remember. My first plants were tiny cacti from the garden centre shelves and jade plants I grew from leaf and tip cuttings from my mother's larger plant. I even planted a bottle garden, inspired by a Ladybird book, with random, hopelessly small plants. I had patchy success, but am still inspired by the seemingly infinite array of plants that will grow inside and the beauty and soul they bring to a house. If I ever need to give the house or my spirits a lift, plant shopping is often the answer.

While I cannot pretend to be the perfect indoor gardener, I have learned which plants are easy and dependable and which are troublesome and demanding. I have also experienced how the right plant, in the right container, is an immensely valuable decorative tool and have developed a pragmatic approach to using plants. Most of the pictures in this book were taken in my homes, with plants and containers featuring in different combinations to demonstrate the range of possible effects that can be achieved. They also demonstrate how plants can be used to provide the finishing touches in interior decorating schemes.

In this book, I hope to share some of what I have learned and inspire you to use more plants to enrich your home with colour and life. As in my garden, I want to use hardworking, good-value plants as much as I can, getting maximum impact for minimum effort and cost, so there is plenty of information on how to match the needs of the plant to the location, the first step to a healthy houseplant. I have also included lists of tough, almost indestructible plants along with suggestions for plants suited to those who just cannot get watering right.

You really do not need to be a dedicated indoor gardener or have green fingers in order to make your home more beautiful with plants. Be inspired by the following pages to bring freshness and vibrant living plants into your home.

Clare Matthews

Designing with houseplants

Houseplants breathe life into an interior: plants lift the spirits, they can provide a burst of colour and rich texture, as well as fill a room with scent and add character. Houseplants are wonderfully versatile, with plants suited to the style and practicalities of just about every room. Used as decorative pieces, living art works or as you might use cut flowers, a few relatively inexpensive, well-chosen plants will reinvigorate a lacklustre room or embellish and enliven a new interior design scheme. The effect of plants on the way a room looks and feels is immense – decorative schemes are softened and rooms made more welcoming by bringing indoors these representatives of the outside world. They are a vibrant link with nature. Teamed with the right container, a houseplant provides the essential finishing touch to any room.

Pot, plant, place

ABOVE *Crammed into a fresh light green basket, these African violets have a country-cottage charm.*

In order to have healthy, fantastic-looking houseplants there are three fundamental points to consider – pot, plant and place. Each point carries equal weight in making a scheme a success, but the absolute ideal starting point is undoubtedly place. Start by looking at a room carefully, considering where a houseplant might add a touch of pizzazz, brighten a dull corner or perhaps soften or disguise some unsightly feature. Then consider what the conditions are like in that position: what sort of light falls there; what is the temperature and does it fluctuate; and is the room dry or humid? Once armed with this information and a good idea about the style of plant that will best suit the room, you are ready to choose the plant.

In reality, most plants are impulse buys, plucked from enticing displays in supermarkets or garden centres. Impossibly green and lush or seductively smothered in a profusion of buds promising to burst into a fantastic floral display, these plants are not always the best investment. Firstly, because they are probably not ideally suited to the places where you really need plants and secondly, because many of these plants are just not a long-term proposition, especially flowering plants shipped in for gift-giving times of the year. Often produced by manipulating the hours of light they receive, these plants are grown in perfect conditions; some are treated with dwarfing chemicals to promote flowering on small plants, all of which means they may be hard to grow on after they have performed once. These plants have their place; a joyful splash of seasonal colour is immensely heartening and they might survive to flower again if you are extremely lucky, but they are not suitable as the mainstay of any scheme.

Other impulse buys result in you wandering around the house, clutching the newly acquired plant, desperately sitting it in possible places and standing back to assess its impact with an appraising eye, only to realize that the conditions in this spot are not right for the plant.

BELOW *The deeply coloured burgundy and chocolate leaves of this begonia set in a pewter-shaded ceramic pot are perfectly in tune with the rich tones of the furnishings of this interior.*

ABOVE *This confident choice of wall colour could diminish the wrong plant but instead the delicate, yet vibrant yellow flowers of this orchid have more presence and more impact because of the bold colour combination.*

In order to get the maximum effect for the least effort, the ideal approach is to choose a plant suited to the specific place, suited in style, habit and needs. Trying to mollycoddle a plant that is not getting what it needs is hard work; it is much easier to choose a specimen that will thrive naturally in the spot you have to fill. Plants from a good supplier are much more likely to be long-lived. Looking at the section on pages 108–121 before you head out to the beguiling nursery displays will help sort out some potential candidates.

Beyond the practical considerations, choosing a plant is much like selecting any other furnishing for your home, its character should suit the room, and its colours and textures work with those of the other elements. Plants have a staggering array of forms and habits – the arching feathery fronds of a delicate fern will have a very different visual impact from that of the tough-looking croton with its brash, variegated leaves, in spite of the fact that they may be a similar size. Most importantly you should like the plant; it seems obvious but there is little fun to be had from living with a plant, perfectly suited to your kitchen windowsill, for example, if you just don't like the way it looks. Taste in plants can be quite personal, some plants may have happy or unfortunate associations; some plants are now considered old-fashioned, like the cheese plant or rubber plant, while others are considered twee. Equally, it may be best to avoid the fashionable 'plants-of-the-moment' simply because fashions change quite rapidly. Ultimately, it seems best to ignore all this and take your inspiration from the plants you like and those that suit your home.

The final element is the container. The potted plant is a partnership between the plant and the container chosen to disguise its plastic pot, and in some respects the appeal of the plant is governed by the style of the pot or container chosen to hold it. The cachepot should obviously suit the plant and the place in shape, size and style. While African violets in a lime-green basket look pretty, fresh and evoke the feel of the country cottage, they may not look their best in a sharp-edged, shiny surfaced modern container. Getting the container and plant partnership right is a balancing act, and both should gain from the partnership.

The photographs on the colour, mood and style pages (see pages 13–19) show how a variety of houseplants and their containers can contribute to the appeal of a number of interiors, from the cool chic of white orchids, through the clean, contemporary appeal of tiny succulents in metallic containers to the jubilantly colourful bowl of spring bulbs and more. With a touch of imagination and experimentation, the possibilities for enhancing your home with houseplants are remarkable and achievable. Plant, pot, place – get this combination right and aesthetic and practical success is assured.

Colour, mood, style

ABOVE *This bowl of glowing tulips immediately attracts the eye, delivering a powerful measure of colour but the way the golden mirrored bowl sits harmoniously with its surroundings stops them looking wildly out of place.*

The three elements of colour, mood and style are inescapably intertwined; the ideal is to manipulate them in harmony to achieve the type of room decor in which you want to live. Colour may help create a mood – often a particular style of decor may lend itself to a specific palette. Houseplants are fantastic, versatile and inexpensive furnishings which, when used with flair, can help to enhance any scheme.

Colour can exude energy, excitement and drama at one end of the scale or harmonious calm and tranquillity at the other. Our emotional response to colour is both personal and shared, a product of individual tastes, experiences and cultural influences. Personal taste, quite rightly, and even fashion will inevitably play some part in the choice of colour and the style of your interior, though plant displays offer a way to make rooms individual, a chance to add

something beautiful or striking with a touch of your own personality. Houseplants deliver a compact, instant punch of colour to enhance any scheme, not just in their rainbow array of blooms but in their fruits, stems, foliage and even the containers in which they are grown. Whether it is a floral decoration on a coffee table echoing a glowing accent colour in the soft furnishings, a beautifully restrained white orchid in an effortlessly chic interior or a delicate, pure green fern softening the hard stone and ceramic edges in a tranquil bathroom, each will improve the atmosphere and character of the room they inhabit.

The colour provided by plants is also useful in manipulating space and focusing attention towards or away from specific elements of a space. Strong bright colours foreshorten a space, instantly seizing the eye. A bold red amaryllis on a windowsill will grab the eye, distracting from the view beyond; set on a table at the centre of the room the same scarlet plant focuses attention away from the edges of room. Use shades of blue where you want to stretch space, since it is the colour that most recedes, giving the impression that a distance is further than it seems. The following pages present an array of images to inspire. They illustrate how everyday houseplants contribute colour, atmosphere and style to interiors.

ABOVE *With a wealth of flower colours available, growing amaryllis is a wonderful way to boost the colour scheme in any room through the winter. The delicate pink of this amaryllis (a* Hippeastrum *hybrid) has been carefully chosen to work with the wall colour*

RIGHT *This maidenhair fern may be a challenge to keep but the perfection of its delicate green foliage is great for softening the harshness of bathroom fittings and surfaces.*

Hot, bold, brilliant

These striking colours always capture attention. They might be used to sound a welcome discordant note in a pale interior or to highlight part of the colour scheme of a room. They are demanding, invigorating and brave, colours so intense you might imagine they actually radiate heat. A startling burst of fiery orange, searing red or brilliant yellow brings energy, excitement and life to any scheme. Housing these plants in a neutral container can dull their impact slightly, but why not use contrasting or similarly coloured pots to really ramp up the impact.

HOT, BOLD, BRILLIANT PLANTS

- Gerbera
- Primula
- African violets
- Tulips
- Lilies
- Bougainvillea
- Anthurium
- Begonias
- Pot chrysanthemums
- Clivia
- Coleus
- Glory lily
- Impatiens
- Kalanchoe
- Poinsettia
- Cinerarias

RIGHT *Like a ball of flame, the flowers of this Clivia burn brightly against the white painted wood. The plain black ceramic pot lets the flower be the star.*

Cool sophisticates

It is not just the elegant muted tones of these plants that earn them a place in this category, their graceful shapes also play a part. To succeed these plants require a stylish container and the whole impression must be one of effortless charm. Blooms of cool white, cream and silver are perfectly suited to an interior where simplicity evokes a luxury and comfort not common to other pared-down or minimal interiors. White and cream orchids and lilies are at once the obvious and the perfect choice, the epitome of chic and restrained glamour. Arching palms, redolent of palm courts, or a tall, narrow-leaved bamboo are well suited to a sophisticated interior where the stolid rubber plant or cheese plant would fail.

ELEGANT PLANTS

- White lilies
- Orchids
- Narrow-leaved bamboos
- Palms
- Umbrella plant
- False aralia
- Ferns
- Aspidistra
- Jasmine
- Most plants with white flowers in the right container

LEFT *Perhaps because it has a cast-iron constituton, the elegance of the aspidistra is often overlooked, yet it is a graceful foliage plant when set in the right container.*

ROMANTIC PLANTS

- Mosaic plant
- Polka-dot plant
- Impatiens
- African violet
- Kalanchoe
- Spring bulbs
- Pelagoniums
- Aluminium plant
- Primulas
- Violets

Pretty romantics

Ceramic bowls, floral jugs and teapots crammed with small flowering plants, baskets laden with pretty foliage like that of the pink polka-dot plant, and worn vintage terracotta planted with spring bulbs, all evoke the cosiness of a country cottage and have a soft, feminine charm. Flower-studded azaleas, dainty cyclamen, jewel-flowered African violets and miniature roses in delicate shades of pink and lavender, grown in fussy vintage china will help to amplify the romantic charms of an interior. Small foliage plants or useful culinary herbs clustered in soft, worn wood will add a fresher note. Keep plants small, grouping them to create impact.

LEFT *Large glass vases encase these striking but extremely spare plants. Grown hydroponically (without soil, in water), these Lucky bamboo are simply pushed into a layer of crushed cockle shells, though any gravel or glass pebbles would work equally well, then water is added to cover the shells.*

BELOW *The clean lines of this metallic container, with its three almost perfectly matched geometric Haworthias mulched in bright white gravel, makes more from less. Alone the plants are small and insignificant; displayed as they are here, the whole thing is a triumph, the perfect adornment for a pared-down interior.*

Crisp contemporaries

The clean lines of a contemporary interior demand equally pared-down bold plants that might almost be exercises in geometry, housed in stark containers. Uncluttered hi-tech interiors, gleaming with metal, stone and leather really benefit from the introduction of life that a plant injects into a room. In this controlled interior, single impressive architectural specimens will have a brilliant effect, as will the almost otherworldly forms of cacti and succulents. Marshalled in orderly rows, perfectly shaped succulents planted in pots severe in their simplicity make the ideal embellishment in these highly contrived interiors. The injection of greens into such a scheme also provides the eye with a fresh focal point.

CONTEMPORARY PLANTS

- Barrel and candle form cacti
- Succulents
- Architectural ferns
- Yuccas
- Dracaenas
- Palms

Tranquil verdure

Green fields, lush woodland, the fresh green of spring – these comforting associations carried by the presence of lush foliage plants in the right setting, enhance an atmosphere of tranquillity and well-being. Amid the hustle and noise of modern life many of us strive to create a sanctuary within our homes, a peaceful haven – for some this might be a serene bedroom or an indulgent bathroom. Healthy green foliage plants set in sympathetically chosen containers will promote this restful mood. Green comes in a myriad of shades, fresh green foliage has the optimism of the arrival of spring, the lush green of palms and tropical plants hints at warmer climes, but avoid dull, lifeless greens like that of the rubber plant. Plants and pots should be simple.

TRANQUIL PLANTS

- Bamboo
- Ferns (especially suited to bathrooms)
- Palms
- Weeping fig

RIGHT *The simplicity and tranquillity of this windowsill display comes from carefully chosen pots and repeated mounds of uncomplicated plants. Mind-your-own-business* (Soleirolia soleirolii) *domes are punctuated by* Kalanchoe *'Magic Bells'.*

Plant position

ABOVE *Bright pink poinsettias in equally brilliant pink pots provide a colourful but unusual take on decorating for Christmas. Seasonal plants are an easy, manageable way to extend the trappings of the festive season into the kitchen.*

Before buying any plants, ideally you will decide which rooms might benefit from the addition of a few environment-enhancing houseplants. Setting aside the matters of colour and style (discussed earlier), there are some practical considerations; chief among these is determining which plants will thrive in the conditions prevailing in the spots you have in mind. It is also worth thinking about scale: large plants cost more to buy, but one good-sized specimen may have more impact and be easier to care for than several smaller ones. Relatively insignificant plants dotted around a large room, such as an open-plan living space, can look lost, whereas if they are grouped en masse on a table or in a fireplace they will have more impact. Intimate spaces, however, are suited to small arrangements, where intricate details of foliage and flowers are best appreciated.

When thinking about how best to use plants to add a touch of pizzazz to your interior decor, practical considerations are important; not just the growing conditions required by the plant, but the space they will occupy. Plants encroaching onto main routes through a room will inevitably get damaged, and the spiky leaves or irritant sap of some potted plants might even damage the perpetrators of the damage. Plants that loll over soft furnishing may cause stains with dropped leaves or faded blooms.

Problem-solving and cover-ups

No interior is perfect: older properties often have visible pipes, boxing or uneven walls, others may have windows looking out onto a neighbour's home or the street. Poorly proportioned rooms can lack height, appear too tall or perhaps just too big to be comfortable. Used thoughtfully, plants offer a low-cost, instant solution to these problems and more.

When tackling problems such as pipes stretching up walls, bumpy plaster and things on the walls you would rather hide, you cannot reasonably expect to completely obscure them. Very few indoor plants would be large enough or dense enough. You are looking for something to soften problem areas so they become insignificant. Select a plant with a fair degree of coverage, which is open and has some movement, something to arrest the eye and distract the onlooker from what lies behind. A Weeping fig or palm would be excellent choices. If you are disguising a strong vertical feature such as pipes or boxing, avoid the obvious temptation to choose a strong vertical plant, like Mother-in-law's Tongue (*Sancevieria*) for example, since this will only draw attention to the pipes as they emerge from behind the foliage.

A light screen of foliage is a gentle way to create privacy at an overlooked window. Light will seep into the room between the leaves and when they are backlit, the leaves will look like a stained-glass window in myriad shades of green. Selected to suit the light levels of the window, the plants can stand on the sill and hang in baskets from the top of the frame. It is also possible to use a delicate climber such as jasmine to provide a fragrant, filigree curtain on a frame or wires at the window. Another approach is to construct a series of shallow shelves across the window to house rows of plants that will cascade and tumble to fill the space.

The right plant can also modify how the proportions of a space are perceived. A powerful vertical plant placed in prominent position, such as a climber trained up a tall support in a room that lacks height, will draw the eye upward, giving the impression that the room is loftier than it is. For spaces with the opposite problem (where large period rooms have been divided into a number of narrower ones, for instance), plants can be ranged on shelves or hung in baskets to lower the ceiling.

BELOW *Leafy palms make a good choice if you want to disguise a particular feature, as the dense cluster of fronds produces shifting patterns and complex shapes. They are also excellent plants for a humid bathroom.*

Large specimens also make excellent diaphanous mobile room-dividers. Large, multifunction, open-plan living spaces are excellent for the communal life of a household but benefit from having clearly defined areas; large plants artfully placed will help delineate areas and break up the space into comfortable chunks. Striking bamboos, palms and even papyrus will work well.

Highlights

A great way to pep up a tired room is to draw attention to its highlights; it may be a fireplace, a charming set of doors or the gorgeous view of the garden beyond. Carefully placed plants are a straightforward way to draw attention to the best features of any room and thus diminish the importance of anything less attractive that might be there as well.

A fireplace is an obvious focal point, the heart of any room; while the fire is burning the hearth is at its most alluring but in the warmer months without the brilliant flames, the fireplace can look dead. A few deftly selected plants can bring it back to life. Like any other ornament, an array of small plants can be used to decorate the mantle shelf – a rank of identical plants, in keeping with the mood of the room, arranged along its length looks striking. Or identical plants at each end should do the trick. Cramming the hearth itself with foliage and flowers makes the fireplace as much of a visual draw as when the fire is lit. The other option is to flank the structure with two impressive plants in equally impressive containers to draw the eye.

Using plants to flank a feature is a simple trick; any doorway, window or piece of furniture immediately gains importance and has its fine features emphasized when given plant sentries. Though the concept is simple, the scale of the plant has to be right to amplify the importance of a window; set, say at waist height, the plants must extend well above this. Another simple strategy to gain the height needed might be to set them on plant stands, stools of even ornate hall chairs – whatever fits in with the style of the room – just to give them the height and presence needed. Generally speaking, flanking a doorway with lower plants will work as the door begins at floor level.

ABOVE *Set in a large doorway where the drawing room meets the conservatory, the sky-blue flowers of this Plumbago mark the transition from one room into another.*

FAR LEFT *Standard French lavenders give prominence to this marble fireplace during the summer when the fire is not likely to be lit.*

The practicalities

If you want a plant that is easy to keep, always looks good and will last for years then simply place it in a spot that is most likely to suit it. How a plant looks in its chosen spot is important, but an unhappy plant will not stay looking good for long. Set in the wrong place a plant may last a few weeks or a few months drawing on its resources, or even struggle on indefinitely, but it will look utterly miserable.

Easily described in terms of light levels, temperature, humidity and frequency of watering, a plant's needs are not always easily met, especially when other influences such as cold draughts and seasonal differences in natural light and heat are drawn into the mix. Homes are generally kept warm and dry, while all plants need a reasonable level of humidity, surprisingly, even cacti. The key factors are the prevailing light levels and temperature; these are

RIGHT *This pretty basket of anemones is probably not in the spot best suited to its needs, but they really pretty up the cloackroom and will only be there until the flowers fade. Once they do, move the plant outside.*

ABOVE *The statuesque* Dracaena marginata *is a very adaptable plant and can be acclimatized to accept a variety of locations from bright indirect light to partial shade.*

RIGHT *Though this traditional fireplace looks wonderfully festive, its display will be short-lived, as the heat from the roaring log fire will not suit the poinsettias even if they are kept well watered. This is an example of choosing to give plants difficult circumstances to grow in and accepting the consequences.*

not easily changed, but it is within your power to control humidity and water supply with misting, pebble trays and regular appropriate watering (see pages 124–27.) Assess the positions you hope to enhance with plants and purchase those that will revel in the prevailing conditions. The plant care profiles give a concise, easy-to-interpret guide to the requirements of each plant (see pages 132–41). If you are unsure, choose an easygoing 'survivor', an unfussy plant that will survive against the odds, though it should be said, they are not indestructible. A number of these stalwart plants, ideal for the nervous and the negligent, are listed on page 110.

The art of display

ABOVE *Three bright-berried Jerusalem Cherry* (Solanum pseudocapsicum) *make a real splash ranged along an antique painted cabinet. This is a very ordinary plant – alone it would not merit much attention, whereas a line of three identical pots makes the display look impressive.*

Making the most of very little is the art of display – taking a few relatively insignificant things and combining them to make something jaw-dropping or surprisingly attractive, considering its constituent parts is a real talent, but you can pick up some useful tips in the next few pages. Good display gives a designed look to a group of objects, a planned arrangement that may look effortless but nonetheless transforms those objects into a coherent whole. There can even be a theatrical, stage-set approach with props pulled in to heighten the drama and increase the impact.

Repetition

The easiest type of arrangement to get right, repetition is a way of making much out of not a great deal. A plant at the centre of a table may have charm once it's noticed, whereas a row of three or five identical tiny pots arranged down the centre of the table looks incredibly special. This linear repetition never fails where there is a linear space to fill – shelves, window ledges, mantle shelves, dressers, table centrepieces – this strategy works for them all.

The rules are simple: the plants and pot must be identical since any aberration would break the spell that the repetition creates; and there must always be an odd number of pots since this looks less contrived and just

RIGHT *A string of tiny, perky violas join forces to magnify their charms. Keep a look out for interesting containers in junk shops and jumble sales – old drinking glasses, pretty jam jars and tea-light containers make wonderful temporary homes for tiny individual plants.*

RIGHT *This simple little trio of two Barrel cacti and a Ponytail palm is united by the metallic pots and their love of the sun.*

LEFT *Clustering these Peperomia plants together gives them the weight of a much larger plant.*

generally nicer and 'right'. (Try even numbers and judge for yourself!) And finally, the spacing must be regular and match the scale of the plants; make the gap too great and the plants are not a group.

Sitting similar plants in identical pots in a group is an alternative form of repetition. Sitting three similar potted plants in a triangular pattern has appeal for many of the same reasons as the liner repetition but gives a more static arrangement. The pots can be so close that the three plants almost merge, though more impact is to be had if they are discernable individuals but close enough together for the grouping to hold. Too much space between them and visually they are not one luxurious group but less significant individuals. More than three plants are not successful displayed in this way.

Groups

When you want something spectacular or need some plant life with real volume, group plants together into one carefully orchestrated display. A few specimens grouped together will have much more impact than the same plants dotted around a room. Large spaces can accommodate a large display of bold plants, but creatively clustering smaller plants on a tabletop or shelf can work equally well.

As well as the advantages of the visual feast you create, displaying plants in choreographed clusters it is also good for the plants. Gathering plants together creates a small microclimate around them, a localized humidity and lessens water evaporation, reducing the need to water. However, it is important to avoid overcrowding and allow air to circulate around the plants as otherwise it can encourage fungal diseases. It is also vital that all the plants you choose enjoy the same living conditions, and demand the same levels of temperature, light and humidity.

Dramatic effect and a sense of luxury are simple to achieve by massing a number of the same plants together in a large bowl or basket. The plants do not need to be exceptional, but piled together they will have real impact, particularly flowering plants.

To build a group of plants either plant them into one large container or put them into a collection of vessels that work together. They do not need to be identical – a group unified by materials, such as a collection of baskets, simple ceramics or stainless steel pots work well and stop the group looking too contrived. Planting subjects in one large container works well for smaller plants but for plants of a reasonable size it becomes impractical. Housing plants in separate pots gives more flexibility, groupings can be arranged and rearranged, members can be added and other moved away. Likewise, flowering plants can be added for a daub of seasonal colour when they are at their peak and then removed once the blooms fade.

Deciding which plants to include could take some time. Colour, texture and form all play a role in how well plants will sit together and each individual needs to be discernable, yet part of the whole. Contrasting textures,

ABOVE *To cheer up a room, gather plants from around the house and tuck them into new containers to form a new focal point. This lively group includes heather, African violets, Peperomia and Flaming Katy.*

RIGHT *Bright pink bracts and blooms might look gaudy under some circumstances, but are successfully tamed here by mellow terracotta pots and off-white furniture.*

colours and leaf size stop the display looking like a nondescript green mound or a chaotic heap. The most straightforward way to decide if you like how your plants look together is to sit them side-by-side and judge the effect. The shape of the group needs to fit the space, but, as a rule, tall subjects stand at the back and others cluster around them. Smaller plants will hide the base of the taller plants. It is worth experimenting with your arrangements, shifting plants around, taking some away or adding others until you find a grouping that is pleasing to your eye and fills the space. Be bold. Don't be afraid to use contrast and colour.

LEFT *Colour, character and geometry make this a cohesive group. Rather cleverly, the yellow theme runs through the basket and pots and the markings on the leaves of the Mother-in-law's Tongue; the shade complements and holds its own when set against the brilliant red Gerbera. The plants all have an association with sun and heat, and the dramatic shape of the cluster works to make this a successful combination.*

RIGHT *Using a prop – a set of shelves, an étagère or in this case, a stepladder with a distressed paint job – kept specifically to show off houseplants can help organize them successfully and provide a permanent but constantly changing decorative display. This array of white pots and plants is restrained, but a more flamboyant and colourful array might follow the same model.*

Big and bold

Using large plants needs a little more thought and planning than smaller specimens. Big plants mean big impact, especially if that plant is in the perfect container for the job. Using a big plant is a bold, confident statement. Large specimens occupy a good chunk of space, they will be expensive because of the time the nursery has invested in production, but the right plant makes an excellent focal point – an instant spectacle to lift a drab room. The cost entailed demands that the big plant you choose will not only look good in the spot you have picked out for it, but that the plant's basic requirements and preferences are met in the location you've chosen. Larger, older plants are more robust than smaller, younger specimens and should be slightly less demanding to care for. Having just one large, beautiful plant in each room can cut down on the time spent on plant care, meaning far fewer plants to water and monitor.

Plants of a good size are best in heavy pots as they can become unstable, especially if their compost dries out, causing damage to themselves and other furnishings as they topple. Keeping significant specimens dust-free so their leaves can function efficiently is difficult; if they are moveable I favour standing them outside in gentle rain every now and again when the temperatures are favourable and there is no cold wind. This really refreshes the plants, and you can almost see the foliage brighten.

Large specimens vary in character; they should be chosen to complement the room's decor and mood. The most practical large plants are those that occupy vertical space rather than those that sprawl or become a nuisance. Climbers such as philodendron or even ivy, trained up a moss pole achieve a good height but occupy little space. The choice of cachepots becomes more limited as plants become larger; you may have to consider pots designed for outdoor use sat in a plant saucer to catch water that drains from the pot, or look creatively at other everyday objects such as wicker log or laundry baskets. Hiding bricks in the base of the pot adds weight and helps to keep the plants stable especially if they are top-heavy.

ABOVE *Neatly clipped standard bays make dramatic houseplants; they have a crisp formality and enjoy the slight subversion of bringing the outdoors in, though an 'occasional holiday' in the garden will undoubtedly improve the health of the plants.*

RIGHT *Gnarled, twisted and worn, this tree is a real marvel. It is a fabulous plant to live with, possessing gravitas and a beauty far greater than many works of art.*

Flower power

There is a real joyfulness about having flowering plants in the house. Their vivacity, colour and verve lift the spirits and delight the eye. With a little work and planning (or regular trips to the garden centre), it is possible to have flowering houseplants decorating your home all year round. Frequent forays to buy seasonal plants may seem lavish but flowering plants are more economical that cut flowers; they provide colour and scent for longer than cut blooms and will probably cost less. There is also the chance (albeit slim with some plants) that you may persuade the plant to flower again with the right care.

ABOVE *Spring bulbs are easy to grow and reliably produce their quota of colourful flowers. There is a fantastic array of blooms to choose from if you plant your own bulbs, but if you don't get around to planting your own, buy them from the garden centre.*

OPPOSITE PAGE *The mop heads of hydrangea (top left) are made up of a host of long-lasting flowers. The exotic blooms of the Glory lily (top right) are borne in profusion throughout the summer. Clivia (bottom left) is easily persuaded to flower again. Available in a rainbow of shades and patterns, the humble viola (bottom right) is an incredibly useful plant for adding a splash of short-term seasonal colour.*

Carefully manipulated to put on a show at just the right time for optimum sales, the seasonal favourites that crowd the shelves at nurseries, garden centres and the supermarket are probably flowering at the 'wrong' time for the plant. The hours of daylight, the temperature, the amount of water and food the plants receive are carefully controlled to make the plants perform. Poinsettias, for example, are treated with dwarfing chemicals and the day length is controlled to ensure they flower to order. This means that although the glorious plant you buy will flower beautifully, it will be very difficult to keep it so that it will flower again. There are always exceptions, the triumphs of dedicated green-thumbed individuals, but for most of us, seasonal flowering plants are a wonderful short-term burst of colour and you should not be disappointed when they subsequently fail to thrive. They, are in essence, disposable plants.

Bowls full of spring bulbs inside herald the optimism that comes with the arrival of spring long before the first green shoots appear outdoors. This is because they have been forced, made to flower earlier than they would do naturally. Hardened off and planted in the garden after the danger of frost has passed, they may flower again. The same goes for plants ordinarily considered outdoor plants that are sold as houseplants when in bloom – plants such as the blousy hydrangea and heathers are good examples. Enjoy them inside for as long as the flowers last, then plant them out in the garden. Equally, when you are in search of some colourful houseplants it is sensible to look at the benches of outdoor plants; those in flower will tolerate a few weeks inside and then they too can be added to the garden.

Unlike the tropical and subtropical exotic plants normally sold as potted plants, garden plants have a more natural appeal and a more direct link to nature and the seasons. In the winter bowed Hellebore flowers are delicate and come in a myriad of colours, while lavenders bring with them the scent of summer. The intense hues of compact heathers are evocative of moorland and wilderness, while primroses and violets are irresistibly pretty; all can be snatched from the outside and enjoyed in the house for a few weeks. Given time to acclimatize and planted out in the garden, they will keep flowering for years. This makes financial sense and it is also more environmentally friendly than disposable seasonal houseplants.

Not all flowering plants have to be short-term visitors; managed correctly some will flower repeatedly, an event eagerly anticipated each year when these long-lived plants can be moved centre stage to be fully enjoyed. This approach highlights one of the problems flowering plants have. Denuded of their buds and blooms once flowering is over they are often too drab to keep the spot they occupied while flowering. You need a suitable, out-of-the-way space to keep them until they are ready to bloom again. My laundry room is often crowded with orchids I am attempting to coax into bloom again.

For the moment

ABOVE *All the joy of long-awaited spring sunshine contained – a goodly sized bowl brimful of daffodils and cowslips herald the onset of spring.*

Many seasonal flowering plants are unlikely to be long-lived but they are the most fantastic quick fix, perfect to add a bit of zing to a lacklustre room, especially if you are expecting guests or are just in need of a pick-me-up. Wedging three or four small, inexpensive flowering plants into a bowl and standing them on a coffee table, kitchen worktop or on a hall table works wonders. In the autumn and winter cyclamen is available. In the spring, muscari, narcissi, tulips and hyacinths bring the scent of spring inside and magnificent amaryllis rise stately from massive bulbs. In the summer the daisy blooms of gerberas blaze with colour and pelargoniums are available in shades of lipstick scarlet to candy-floss pink. Place these plants where they are seen to best effect, keep them watered and tidy by picking off spent flowers that might ruin the effect. In general, blooms will last longer in cooler rooms; left in a hot spot with insufficient water, flowers soon fade.

AMARYLLIS (most sold are in fact *Hippeastrum*): Bold and magnificent, the clusters of brilliantly coloured trumpets that form atop thick hollow stems make a real impact. Each stem will produce three or four large blooms and if you are lucky each bulb will send up a second flower spike. Growing amaryllis is like watching a slowly unfolding drama that you know will come to an amazing crescendo. Once the flowers have faded it is all over; remove the flower stalk and pop the pot of strap-like leaves in an out-of-the-way place and feed and water until autumn. This is important to build up reserves for next year's dramatic show. Then withhold water in the autumn; the foliage will shrivel and you need to leave the bulb to rest for a couple of months before you begin watering again to repeat the process. I have included amaryllis in the one-time-only list because it is tricky to get the bulb to perform as well as it did the first time.

CINERARIA (*Senecio cruentus*): Always bought in bloom, the plant itself is obscured under a dome of intensely coloured, daisy-like flowers. Once the flowers are over the plant is spent and ugly. It enjoys good light but prefers cool temperatures, and the compost should be kept moist.

BULBS: Easy and effective, most of the hard work in persuading a bulb to produce flowers will have been done by the nurseries in preparing them for sale. All you have to do is plant and water them or sit them in some water. If you do not quite get around to buying bulbs at the right time, cheat and buy them already growing, but well before they come into bloom. Fed to restore the energy they have expended in flowering and acclimatized to conditions outdoors, bulbs can be planted out in the garden after flowering.

GERBERA (*Gerbera*): A large genus, and like many of the plants on this list, gerbera is a perennial but the plants are more commonly purchased for an instant though temporary splash of colour. The leaves are unremarkable but the blooms are happiness on a stalk. They like sun, humidity and warmth.

POINSETTIA (*Euphorbia pulcherrima*): What appear to be colourful 'petals' are actually bracts of this seasonal plant – the flower is the tiny structure at the centre. In the run-up to the Christmas holiday, shops and garden centres are full of poinsettias; for many people this plant is an essential part of decorating their home for the holidays. The hours of light the plants receive in the run-up to Christmas will be carefully controlled to ensure they flower at just the right moment. The bracts come in the most traditional hard red, through softer pinks to elegant greenish white. This plant needs reasonable

ABOVE *With a disposition almost as sunny as its flowers, gerbera will throw up new flowers for weeks given a modicum of care.*

light and a fairly cool room, around 18°C (64°F) and it will not tolerate draughts. Persuading the plant to flower again requires extreme dedication, since it must not receive any more than 10 hours of light for two months to trigger flowering. Any light will disturb the process. It is easier to buy new plants each year or use something else for a blast of seasonal colour.

CYCLAMEN (*Cyclamen persicum*): Possessed of pretty flowers and decorative marbled leaves, the cyclamen is a popular flowering plant, available through the autumn and winter. The miniature cyclamen is a more delicate, useful plant than its slightly brash, larger incarnation. Cyclamen enjoy a cool room in a light position – anything over 15.5°C (60°F) is too warm. The plant grows from a corm that should be kept dry when watering (water the soil not the corm), the compost should be kept moist during flowering and a feed given every two weeks. Once blooming has finished the plant can be put in a cool site in the garden. You may be lucky and keep the plant going, but getting more flowers may be harder. Miniature cyclamens are more tolerant of warmer temperatures and are generally easier to manage.

GARDENIA (*Gardenia jasminoides*): Marvellously chic, the fragrant, creamy blooms of this gardenia are set against its dark, glossy foliage. It is a charming plant often given as a gift. It is, however, notoriously difficult to keep. Most 'instant' flowering plants generally last trouble-free until they stop flowering, but with the gardenia even that is not a given. Too wet, too cold, too hot or too great a temperature swing and the flower buds will fall off. Leaves will yellow if watered with hard water or if its roots are too cold, so use only tepid soft water. It needs very high light levels but no direct sun and an even 15.5–18°C (60–65°F). Good luck!

GLORY LILY (*Gloriosa superba* 'Rothschildiana'): This fabulously exotic climber produces glamorous blooms with flame-like red petals that fade to yellow at the centre of the flower, and fascinating leaves that taper to a tendril at their tip. Usually sold trained onto a loop of wire, the 2 metre (7 ft) long shoots grow anew each year from a tuber, like a dahlia. The plant enjoys a warm spot but not in direct sun, and plenty of water in the growing season. Feed once a week. Once the flowers have faded give less water and when the growth withers store the tuber in a dry place at around 18°C (65°F). In the spring begin watering again, provide a temperature of around 21°C (70°F) and the tubers should sprout once again. If you are lucky, the tuber may divide, producing two plants.

For every season

ABOVE *The starry blue flowers of the half-hardy* Isotoma axillaris *are more commonly found on the terrace, but these small plants are a great choice for decorating the house in summer.*

Specific flowers are immediately redolent of a particular season and bringing them into your home provides a link to the rhythms of the natural world. It also offers you a chance to reinvigorate an interior by adding a new burst of colour and perhaps scent as the seasons change. The following pages offer suggestions for all the seasons.

Spring

One of the real joys of having spring plants inside is that it allows spring to come early. While outdoors in the garden, bulbs may just be poking their first shoots above the bare soil, inside a carnival of colours and scents will fill the house with the welcome sense that better weather is on its way. Though many bulbs have a cottage-garden appeal, they will enliven any style of room.

If you are organized it is easy to grow your own bulbs, planting them in the autumn and keeping them in a cool, dark place until the shoots are about 5 cm (2 in) high and then bringing them into the light. Otherwise, nurseries and garden-centre shelves are brimful with pots containing two or three bulbs as soon as the winter holiday season is over. Choose those bulbs with good strong growth, that are just a few centimetres (inches) tall, that way you will have the pleasure of watching them grow. If the buds are already open you will only be enjoying them for a week or so. To prolong flowering, keep bulbs in a cool room. Once the flowers have faded and outdoor frosts have passed, the bulbs can be acclimatized and planted in the garden. Give them some general-purpose feed and they may flower again next year.

Bulbs are not the only option if you want to bring the special cheeriness of spring inside – primulas, azaleas and violas will all carry the magic of the season indoors.

SPRING FLOWERS

- Hyacinths
- Narcissus
- Muscari
- Tulips
- Crocus
- Violas
- Primulas
- Azaleas

LEFT *I felt the jewel-like tiny flowers of the crocus deserved an equally opulent setting so I gilded a tiny urn to make a sumptuous show for spring.*

SUMMER FLOWERS

- Marguerites
- Lavender
- Geraniums
- Pelargoniums
- Freesia
- Gerbera
- Italian Bellflower
- Flame lily
- Heliotrope
- Impatiens
- Hydrangea
- Dwarf sunflowers
- Calla lilies

Summer

In the summer, there are plenty of flowering plants from which to choose. Plants sold as garden plants will happily do a stint inside while they are at their best. Once the blooms have faded they can be planted in the garden, making them excellent value for money. Put a flowering shrub or sub-shrubs like lavender or simple Marguerite daisies in a pretty pot at the centre of the kitchen table and you have the uplifting essence of summer right there. Even many of the annuals sold for seasonal pots and containers outside will flower happily indoors.

Autumn

Some summer blooms persist into the autumn, while other new plants are coming to the fore – pelargoniums and fuchias flower well into the autumn. In constructing a display for autumn it is the need for colour that comes to mind, since the season is strongly linked to the rich rusts, oranges and scarlet of falling leaves. Chrysanthemums, good old-fashioned pot mums, come in a range of colours including rusty browns and yellows. I am not sure they can be brought up-to-date, but they suit a cosy cottage or vintage interior. A more fashionable plant is the Kangaroo Paw plant, its unusual flowers are orange through to scarlet held amongst fabulous tactile foliage.

AUTUMN FLOWERS

- Cyclamen
- Chrysanthemums
- Cineraria
- Kangaroo Paw
- Ornamental brassicas

Winter

Most gardens look their worst at this time of year, everything but the evergreens are dormant. So the glossy unchanging foliage of plants inside is very welcome as are the profusion of flowering plants destined to become gifts or decorations for the festive season. Most of these plants will be very hard to keep once they have flowered. Filling the house with plants studded in richly coloured flowers throughout the winter lifts the spirits and captures the mood of the season. South-facing windowsills that receive too much sun for most plants in the summer can now be decorated with flowering plants. Ensure plants are not chilled at night, especially if they are behind heavy curtains. Cooler rooms will suit cyclamen and the Christmas cactus. Including potted plants in your decorations for the holiday season allows you create a special display in each room.

WINTER FLOWERS

- Amaryllis
- African violet
- Cyclamen
- Cineraria
- Poinsettia
- Christmas cactus
- Winter-flowering heather

FAR LEFT *The host of fluttering blooms held over the marbled foliage of dainty cyclamen should last for several weeks.*

RIGHT *The soft creamy bracts of this pale poinsettia cultivar in its restrained cachepot lend the plant charm and elegance that extend beyond the festive season.*

Bringing the outside in

There are a number of flowering garden plants that lend themselves to the indoor treatment. Once they have finished flowering indoors, it is generally time to put them back outside where they will be happiest. Primroses and hydrangeas, heathers and hellebores all make great visitors to the indoor landscape. But don't stop there – look at your topiary, bay trees and lavenders for the indoor treatment, too.

PRIMROSE (*Primula vulgaris*): Arranged like a perfect sweet posy of flowers framed by crinkled leaves, the simple charm of the primrose is easily spoiled if you cram one of every colour into the same basket. Primulas seemingly come in all colours of the spectrum, and though there are some pastel hues, many are strident and do not combine comfortably. To mix the colours successfully, use care and stick to two colours to make it simple; filling a large bowl with just one colour of plant also guarantees success. Keep the plants moist and in a cool spot. Pinch out fading flowers to keep the plants looking fresh. After blooming, primulas can be planted out in the garden where they may appear year after year.

HYDRANGEAS (*Hydrangea*): Gaudy in blues and pinks but elegant in pure white, the flowers of the hydrangea have real bulk and impact. A cool location will suit the plant best and though sold as houseplants they are best planted outside when finished blooming.

HEATHERS (*Erica and Calluna*): This evergreen garden perennial is a common sight in nursery outdoor displays in the winter as it is one of the few plants that blooms at this time of year (though some cultivars flower at other times of the year). In shades of pink and white, these plants can be used as houseplants while they are in flower for a dash of uplifting colour and then planted in the garden after a period of acclimatization to the conditions outside. The plant will fare best in a cool room and the blooms will last longer. Keep the compost moist using rainwater as this is an acid-loving plant.

HELLEBORES (*Helleborus*): The nodding flowers of the hellebore are a real delight especially coming as they do when the winter is at its bleakest. In the garden, the pretty downward-facing flowers are easily overlooked. The traditional Christmas rose is white but hellebores are also available in dusky pinks, yellows and sophisticated blacks and purples. Buy them just before they are in full bloom, keep the plant inside in a cool position where the exquisite flowers can be appreciated and then plant out in a shady spot in the garden after hardening them off.

LAVENDERS (*Lavandula*): Bringing pots of flowering lavender into a room delivers one of the essential scents of summer into your home. Water sparingly and cut off the spent flower stalks to use in the linen cupboard or potpourri and return the plant to the garden where it will flower for years.

TOPIARY: Although these are not flowering plants, box and yew plants that have been shaped into spheres, cones or lollipops, can look very stylish in the right interior, especially gracing a hallway or entranceway. They will tolerate draughts that may kill more tropical houseplants; however, they should only come indoors for a short while before spending time outside to recuperate (domestic houses are too warm for these outdoor-loving plants). Bringing potted specimens in from the garden to flank doorways is an ideal way to add a touch of pizzazz when dressing the house for a party.

TOP *Neatly tucked into a recycled lined gift box with a small variegated ivy, two small primulas make a big impression. Green is an excellent foil for most colours, though the exact shade can make a big difference.*

ABOVE *Placing a flowering hellebore on a high shelf or mantelpiece allows the subtle beauty of its downward-facing flowers to be fully appreciated.*

Enduring blooms

There are a number of hardworking houseplants that have a long flowering period and will reward you with copious and continuous blooms. The following pages suggest a huge range of plants that will bloom and bloom, making them economical and beautiful options when buying houseplants. African violets, Christmas cactus, orchids of various kinds, jasmines and roses are all possibilities if you are looking for plants that will continue to put on a glorious show for weeks and weeks.

LEFT *It takes very little trouble to keep an African violet growing and flowering for years. As well as being obliging plants, their intensely coloured flowers have an instant appeal, especially when crowded together in the same container.*

RIGHT *This perfect white orchid has great style and elegance. Wherever they are placed, orchids add a touch of instant glamour and hold their flowers for months with little care, making them a great decorating solution.*

ORCHIDS: Perfect, graceful flowers held over the most ordinary of foliage, these hard-working plants produce lavish flower spikes that last for months. With a dependable, easy glamour, orchids are a great personal favourite and they never fail to add a touch of style to a room (see pages 60–63 for more details on orchid care).

CHRISTMAS CACTUS (*Schlumbergera*): An old favourite, this cactus should produce a profusion of blooms over the holiday period in unbridled shades of red, pink, purple and a more serene white. To ensure your plant flowers, move it to a cool location and reduce the amount of water for about four weeks, then move to a warmer spot, step up the watering and feed when buds form. This plant benefits from a holiday outside in the summer in a warm, semi-shaded position. If this plant is happy, it will grow into a monster and go on flowering year after year, rarely needing potting on.

ABOVE *Although normally known for its fiery orange flowers, Clivia also has a delicate yellow cultivar that may better suit some decorating schemes.*

RIGHT *This Kalanchoe was one of the plants I gave my daughter when she went off to university, and here it is home again for the summer when others did not make it.*

AFRICAN VIOLET (*Saintpaulia*): Small jewel-like flowers nestle amongst velvety leaves for months. This is one of the easiest flowering plants to keep if it has all it requires. It enjoys good, indirect light – an east-facing windowsill is ideal – and only needs watering when the top of the compost is dry. Use tepid water, taking care to water the compost rather than the plush leaves, as droplets will cause damage. Some people find it easier to water this plant by standing it in a tray of water until the compost is damp.

JASMINE (*Jasminum officinale*): This scrambling climber can be grown successfully inside in a sunny room or conservatory, and is used to clothe walls, trellises or trained up an obelisk. In summer keep the compost fairly moist, but in winter just keep the plant from drying out. The heady fragrance of a good-sized jasmine contained within a conservatory or sunny room is incredibly powerful, so consider whether you enjoy the fragrance or not.

KANGAROO PAW (*Anigozanthos*) This native of Australia gets its name from the shape and hairiness of its flowers. It has lance-shaped leaves and flowers from late spring to mid-summer, and enjoys a bright site but not full sun, a good supply of soft water throughout the summer and non-alkaline fertilizer. Restrict its water in winter. It can be placed outdoors in the summer, though this may mean missing its flowering inside.

FLAMING KATY (*Kalanchoe blossfeldiana*): Available most of the year and always sold with a good crop of flowers in punchy shades of pink, red, yellow and orange, this plant is very easy to keep, flowering again and again and again. As it is a succulent, it needs little water, feeding just once or twice a year and enjoys a warm bright situation.

BOUGAINVILLEA (*Bougainvillea*): Redolent of Mediterranean climes, the intense colours associated with this plant come from red, pink, violet and orange bracts rather than flowers. Best suited to the conservatory, this sprawling, thorny plant is easy to grow and long-lived. It requires only weak feed in the summer and needs to be fairly dry and cool in the winter to bloom well. Trim in the spring.

CALLA LILY (*Zantedeschia*): The 'flower' of the Calla lily is, in fact, a large spadix (a spike inflorescence) swathed in a lavish bract. It has lush green arrow-shaped leaves and does best in a bright or slightly shaded position. Throughout the growing season it requires plenty of water and feeding until it blooms. After flowering, withhold water and fertilizer and allow the tuber to rest until early spring when it can be potted on and the process begun again.

BUSH LILY (*Clivia miniata*): Once the dazzling orange or yellow flowers atop the hollow stem fade, chunky seedpods will form if you allow them. Though attractive, they sap the strength of the plant and reduce the likelihood of repeat flowering. Cut the flower spike out leaving the strap-like leaves. Keep cool and dry in the dormant period until flower spikes form again, then move to a warmer spot and begin feeding when the flower spike reaches full height.

Enduring blooms

AZALEAS (*Azalea indica*): Often sold smothered in delicate blooms, azaleas are woody, shrubby plants with tough-looking foliage. They should, in theory, be long-lived plants but they are not that easy to keep going after blooming. These plants require acid soil, prefer to be watered with rainwater and if you move them to a larger pot, use ericaceous compost. They enjoy cool conditions in a shaded spot. After blooming and after the risk of frost has passed, these plants can be placed in the garden for the summer. If the leaves become yellow it is likely the plant is short of iron – a specialist fertilizer should put this right. If forced to bloom to make an appealing purchase the plant will revert to its natural flowering rhythm.

CRANE FLOWER, BIRD OF PARADISE (*Strelitzia*): Statuesque and exotic, this striking plant is long-lived but requires careful management. To flower each year in spring and early summer, it needs to be pot-bound, requires regular feeding and careful watering in the summer, although it prefers free-draining soil and should never be allowed to sit in water. In winter it should be kept above 10°C (50°F) and fairly dry. If the weather is warm enough the plant will enjoy being outside and can be acclimatized to full sun.

LEFT *In full bloom this pure white azalea provides an excellent welcoming note in a cool hallway.*

RIGHT *The exceptional* Heliconia *'Olympic Dream' will thrive in a brightly lit, warm spot, producing a steady flow of unusual long-lasting flowers throughout the summer.*

MINIATURE ROSES (*Rosa*): The dainty blooms of the very dwarfed rosebush are sadly lacking in fragrance, which would, of course, be wonderful. Not perhaps to everyone's taste, these plants are often an inexpensive impulse or gift purchase, but they will flower throughout the summer if fed regularly and the compost is kept barely moist. Do not sit the plant in water though, as this encourages root rot. Regular deadheading will keep the blooms coming; using scissors, snip off the spent blooms just above the next set of leaves. In the spring cut back any straggly growth so the plant has a pleasing shape and it may well carry on growing.

SCENTED GERANIUM (*Pelargonium*): Evocative of the cottage garden, the leaves of these plants are prettily shaped and scented like roses, lemons and mint. The flowers are delicate, pastel colours and appear throughout the summer if the plant has been allowed a cool period in the winter at around 8–12°C (46–54°F). This is the perfect plant to keep in terracotta pots stood on vintage saucers, crammed on a sunny kitchen windowsill.

PEACE LILY (*Spathiphyllum*): The graceful spadix and spathe of the *Spathiphyllum* is held aloft on an improbably thin stem over glossy foliage. These stately blooms are not typical flowers but they are characteristic of the Arum family and will last for weeks if not months. When the plant ceases to bloom the leaves are attractive enough to hold their own. This is a tropical plant so it enjoys a warm, humid atmosphere and will tolerate bright indirect light to a more shaded position. Feed regularly in the summer.

STEPHANOTIS (*Stephanotis floribunda*): The dark, leathery leaves of this twining plant are the ideal foil for its waxy, tubular white flowers, which are not only beautiful but scented too. Normally sold trained on a wire hoop framework on the verge of flowering, these are popular gift plants and can be found forced into bloom outside their usual flowering time from late spring and summer. Keeping them going can be a real tussle. They require very good indirect light, watering with soft water, warmth and a humid atmosphere. Misting regularly is ideal. Water less frequently in the winter; just keep the compost very slightly moist.

CAPE PRIMROSE (*Streptocarpus*): With the right care, hard-working *Streptocarpus* should flower from spring right through to early winter, year after year. The most likely cause of reduced flowering is over-potting, too little light or incorrect feeding. The plants require a good bright location but not direct sun, which will scorch the leaves. Over-watering can also cause difficulties so ensure the surface of the compost dries before you water or the roots may rot. Remove spent flowers and dying leaves and in winter reduce watering and stop feeding. Though these plants will continue for a number of years, older ones tend to get a little scruffy-looking. With the numerous modern hybrids now available there is a large range of colours to choose from.

Enduring blooms 57

PLUMBAGO (*Plumbago caerulea*): The clear, sky-blue of the Plumbago is arguably the perfect blue flower while the white form is cool and serene. The plant is gloriously generous with its flowering and given the right conditions it will bloom from spring right through to the autumn. I recommend that you snipping off dead flowers before they drop; I have known the fallen, spent blooms of the blue cultivar to stain a pale carpet with little blue specks. Water generously in the summer, feeding once a week, and keep the compost just damp in the winter. The growth can be unbalanced and rather ungainly as it produces long stiff shoots that seem to jut out at odd angles, so a quick tidy-up with the secateurs in the winter will keep it looking good. A well-lit position really suits Plumbago, which makes it an ideal conservatory plant. Its frothy blue flowers lend it a cottagy feel so the plant will look fantastic displayed in a wicker log basket. Make sure that you choose a basket large enough to hold a plant saucer to catch the drips!

LEFT *The exquisitely marked flowers of this Streptocarpus cultivar are so delightful, it is hard to believe that this little plant could continue to produce more of the same for months.*

RIGHT *Blue can be a cold, hard and unwelcoming colour, but this prolific Plumbago somehow manages to produce blooms that have a softness perfectly complementing the colour scheme in this shaded conservatory.*

Exotic orchids

Orchids are special. Nothing looks more elegant, more chic and more
luxurious than a simple ceramic bowl crammed with delicious white orchids.
These are one of the plants people become 'hooked' on; the exquisite beauty
of their flowers is beguiling and there are rare and precious plants to be
collected and acquired. Orchids are sometimes seen as hard to keep and costly
but while this is true of some, the *Phalaenopsis* and *Cymbidium* orchids are
fantastically floriferous and undemanding.

The orchid's reputation as a difficult plant to care for may stem from the great numbers of inexpensive small orchids available in supermarkets and garden centres that fail to thrive beyond flowering. Forced into bloom, the plant is weakened and so can be hard to maintain. Even so these plants offer terrific value, the flowers last between eight and 12 weeks, a phenomenally good-value plant when compared to cut flowers.

Phalaenopsis orchids

The *Phalaenopsis* (Moth) orchid is the easiest orchid to keep, closely followed by the *Cymbidium* (Boat) orchid. They are less expensive than the others, but still have a restrained perfection that gives orchids their appeal. I use them in just about every room in a whole range of colours, slipped into cachepots that

vary in character. They never fail to attract the eye, and they have so much presence that their size is unimportant. These are fantastic houseplants.

Phalaenopsis orchids are usually planted in an orchid bark rather than compost; this very free-draining mix helps avoid over-watering. They are epiphytes in the wild and so this growing medium suits them. Water only when the bark compost is almost dry and never leave the pot sitting in water. Many cachepots specifically designed for orchids have a lip around the inside so the orchid will never sit in water that drains through (unless it is watered excessively). Feed with special orchid food following the manufacturer's instructions in the summer. Orchids appreciate occasional misting and do well in the humidity of a bathroom.

Do not be alarmed if white roots protrude from the bark and the plant appears to be literally climbing out of the pot. The roots need air and it prefers to be a little pot-bound; when you move it to a larger pot, every two or three years, only give it a little more space each time. You will invariably buy your *Phalaenopsis* orchid with one or two flower spikes – when these are spent cut the flower spike off at the first node, (this is a bump in the stem), below the faded blooms. A new flower spike should grow from this point. This orchid enjoys indirect easterly light and to ensure flowering, the night-time and daytime temperatures need to vary by 10–15°C (50–59°F). If it is slow to flower, try moving it to a colder spot, about 5°C (41°F) for three or four weeks and then raise the temperature again. The only downside of this glorious orchid is that when it is not in flower, its stumpy leaves have little going for them, so plants need to be moved into a suitably inobtrusive space until they flower again.

Cymbidium orchids

With flowers that are not quite as long-lived as the Moth orchid, the *Cymbidium* (or Boat) orchid is almost as straightforward to care for – the flowers have real staying power, blooming for a good two months. Their blooms are a little flashier, a little more waxy and exotic-looking and as many as twenty can be ranged up a single stalk. It has long slender leaves that arch gracefully. These can become very large plants, though there are miniature cultivars. They need moderate watering, allowing the compost to dry out a little each time and ensuring the plant is not sitting in water. They will enjoy a warm, humid atmosphere, so occasional misting will help keep the plant looking its best. After flowering cut the flower spike from the plant at its base; when it next flowers a new spike will grow. Feed with specialized orchid fertilizer as per the manufacturer's instructions. Repot every two to three years in a compost specifically designed for orchids, and do not give them too much more space in the new pot, as they enjoy being a little cramped.

Other orchids

The hybrids of the ravishing Tiger orchids are straightforward while the species Tiger orchid is best left to the experts. *Oncidium* orchids are epiphytic, have literally hundreds of species and their requirements vary considerably; some will require temperatures found in a hot house, while others will do well at room temperature. *Oncidium* 'Rotkappchen' is often available with its small yellow- and brown-marked flowers; it does well in similar conditions to the Moth orchid in my experience.

The Lady's Slipper orchid (*Paphiopedilum*) is entrancing, and its flowers are a feast for the eyes but they require an enormous amount of care and nurturing, too much for most people. In reality, you are unlikely to run the risk of buying choice and difficult orchids unless you seek them out. If you do succumb to the passion of the orchid collector, there are many detailed volumes on the subject.

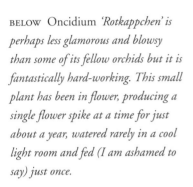

BELOW Oncidium *'Rotkappchen' is perhaps less glamorous and blowsy than some of its fellow orchids but it is fantastically hard-working. This small plant has been in flower, producing a single flower spike at a time for just about a year, watered rarely in a cool light room and fed (I am ashamed to say) just once.*

RIGHT *Illuminated by the light from the window, these orchid flowers glow. This plant would not be scorched, even in a warm sunny window.*

Heavenly scent

ABOVE *The fresh flowers and sweet scent of Stephanotis make it a welcome guest in a small cloakroom.*

With some flowering houseplants comes the luxury of scent. Some blooms, like the hyacinth, are fragrant enough to fill a room with their scent, while others are more subtle, noticed only as one walks passed. Like colour, scent is a matter of personal taste and experience. Most light, natural floral fragrances are unlikely to offend, though the full-on, heady scent of a bowl of hyacinths or lilies might be heavenly to most people, but cloying to a few. Put scented plants where passing people will stir the air, wafting the scent into the room.

RIGHT *Hyacinths produce one of the strongest fragrances of all the flowers you might choose to grow in your home. Just a few blooms will fill a room with their sweet scent.*

CITRUS PLANTS (*Citrus*): The waxy blossoms and the foliage of citrus plants are scented with the fragrance of warmer climes. A long-lived plant, the citrus should deliver deliciously scented blossom every year. The flowers are small, waxy and pretty but not eye-catching. Their scent, however, is outstanding.

HYACINTHS AND LILIES: Both produce a short-lived show of powerfully scented, beautiful flowers. The forced bulbs can be planted in the garden after flowering once they have been acclimatized to conditions outside to possibly flower again the following year.

JASMINE (*Jasminum*): This climber has a powerful scent. It is a large plant, which is best grown in a conservatory where it can easily cover the walls. The scent of jasmine is one that some people may find difficult to bear and may induce headaches in some individuals.

STEPHANOTIS (*Stephanotis floribunda*): A climbing plant often sold trained on a wire hoop, just as it is about to bloom. The flowers are elegant white trumpets with a star-shaped end and stand out well against the dark green foliage. The scent is quite delicate.

Fabulous foliage

Fabulous foliage plants always look good – when you invest in a houseplant with magnificent foliage, you are buying constancy and a permanent furnishing as long as you treat it well. Flowering plants may be alluring but their blooms are often fleeting, so generally speaking, foliage plants are much easier to keep and better value than flowering plants. Most foliage plants obviously do flower – ferns being the notable exception – but the leaves and structure are what make foliage plants interesting. As these plants are permanent residents in your home rather than fleeting seasonal visitors, choosing the right specimen for a particular spot is vital, but with an array of colours, textures and forms to chose from, there are foliage plants to suit every room, whatever its character, decor or mood.

From lush paddle-shaped banana leaves, the intricate lacy fronds of delicate ferns to starkly geometric succulents and spiny cacti, the variety amongst foliage plants is staggering. Just as plants have evolved to survive in just about every climate around the globe, so there must be one equipped to thrive just where you need an uplifting injection of green (or yellow or purple in some cases). As a very rough rule of thumb (and like all useful rules there are exceptions), if the leaves of a foliage plant look tough, then the plant is generally tough and tolerant too. Lush, fragile foliage generally belongs to less robust plants.

ABOVE LEFT AND ABOVE *Though small, the conspicuous textures and glowing colours of the leaves make this Peperomia a stand-out plant when set in a container chosen to amplify its charms.*

Variegation

Foliage plants are not necessarily green – there are delightfully patterned leaves, sparkling variegations and a rainbow of subtle shades of green. Indeed, some of the variegations and leaf colours available are so outlandish they appear fake and far gaudier than any lurid flower might be. The Croton (*Codiaeum*) is one such plant; in some varieties its spectacularly colourful shiny leaves, daubed with yellow, green and red are not for the faint-hearted. Nor the strident pink, crimson and lime-green foliage of the Coleus, so busy it can be hard to place successfully. In fact, variegated plants should perhaps come with a 'handle-with-care' label; some have so much colour, pattern and texture shoehorned into one leaf they can be hard to live with. Variegations are also very difficult to mix; as a rule I would include no more than one variegated plant in a group, as the resulting patterns from combining plants

RIGHT *The leaves of the Croton are streaked and daubed with a raucous array of colours.*

can look confused and just plain messy. Pretty or subtle variegations, such as those of the Weeping Fig (*Ficus benjamina* 'Starlight'), are much easier to use, while brassy, splodge-covered leaves may be colourful but tend to lack charm and appear too contrived to look good.

Begonias, in their darker varieties, have almost velvety-covered leaves. Seldom individually named, these plants are available with an array of staggering patterns on their leaves. They have a reputation for being a little old-fashioned perhaps, but the dark-leaved varieties, can look sumptuous. The rich chocolate- and claret-coloured plants make a splendid foil for white flowered plants in a grouping. Another incredibly useful variegated plant is the humble ivy (*Hedera*); a real survivor, this robust plant has endless colourful variations and though the larger-leaved plants can look a little loud, the smaller, starry-leaved cultivars, streaked and marbled with white, cream, yellow and silver, are really very dainty. Trained up a moss pole, allowed to cascade from shelves and furniture or used to accompany flowering plants, ivies are inexpensive, versatile survivors.

On a practical level, it is important to get the light levels for variegated plants right. In nature, colourful variegations evolved as an adaptation to the amount of light available to the plant; the green part of the leaf is the only area that contains chlorophyll and photosynthesizes, producing energy. The exceptions are pink and red leaves, which use light from a different part of the spectrum. The Coleus and Croton need bright light, while the Mosaic plant (*Fittonia*) need to be kept out of direct sunlight to thrive.

BELOW LEFT *Ivy is available in a vast array of variegations; although rarely named, look for those with cream and light green markings that lend a brightness to the leaves and will lighten a dull corner.*

BELOW *The aptly named* Begonia rex *'l'Escargot's leaves are fascinating; their colour and structure combine to form a spiral.*

Foliage plants

The Asparagus fern is a light, elegant and airy plant whose foliage looks best cascading down from a shelf or mantelpiece.

In the following pages you will find a number of houseplants noted for their attractive foliage: some have particularly striking leaf forms, others are distinguished by their dramatic size, and still others are endowed with interesting colour or shape. Among them will be at least one to suit most decorative schemes and lighting situations.

AFRICAN MASK, AMAZON LILY (*Alocasia amazonica*): The markings on the leaves of the *Alocasia* are so striking and the leaves so perfect that they almost look too good to be real (see a wonderful example on page 66). The arrow-shaped leaves often have a metallic sheen with the veins marked out clearly. It grows best in a partially shaded, humid and warm spot and requires a temperature of at least 18.5°C (65°F) even in the winter. Water with soft water, keeping the compost moist and feed every couple of weeks.

ASPARAGUS FERN (*Asparagus setaceus* and *A. densiflorus*): This plant is not a true fern, though its fine feathery foliage has earned it its common name. It is actually a member of the lily family. The Asparagus fern will tolerate any situation from good light to slight shade, but will scorch in direct sunlight. The growing medium should be kept reasonably moist, but not wet through the growing season and just moist in the winter. The plant can get a little untidy but responds well to being cut back to keep it in shape.

BEGONIA (*Begonia rex*): Here I refer to the coloured-leaf begonias (*Begonia rex*), rather than those grown for their flowers. A number of begonias have been bred with an amazing array of leaf colours and patterns ranging from fresh lime-green, through genuine pinks to deep chocolates and rich, velvet browns. The colours are spread in intricate patterns across the leaf surface, each of the many leaves on the plant sporting an almost identical pattern. There are many named cultivars but those found in garden centres are seldom labelled. The compost should be kept moist all year round and though the plant requires a humid atmosphere it should not be misted; stand it on a pebble tray, though the pot should not sit in the water. It requires less water in the winter.

CALATHEA (*Calathea*): This impressive genus of tropical plants need warm temperatures and plenty of humidity, water and bright indirect light or slight shade to look their best, and feeding every couple of weeks. In winter, it needs less water and does not tolerate draughts. There are various cultivars but all have splendidly marked leaves so a simple, plain ceramic container or basket is all that is needed to make a striking display. This is the perfect plant for a conservatory that is heated in winter.

SPIDER PLANT (*Chlorophytum comosum*): Everyone at some time has probably owned a Spider plant, probably because the plant is incredibly easy to propagate and may have been a gift from a keen indoor gardener. As an ubiquitous plant it is often overlooked, but it is easy to care for, and when used in the right way can look very exciting. The plant has a strong architectural form and is generally very inexpensive to buy (if you don't have a friend with a plant festooned with plantlets), so is a great choice for creating a linear repetition for maximum impact. The fountain of fresh green-and-white-variegated foliage is accompanied by plantlets sent out on long, arching runners. These actually add to the plant's appeal, however, too many small

ABOVE *Teamed with a fresh green cachepot, the foliage of the humble Spider plant appears bright and interesting.*

LEFT *The splendidly marked leaves of this Calathea are typical of the group, and a simple container is all that is needed to show them off. Diffuse light and high humidity are required to keep the plant happy.*

plants left on the 'mother' plant will sap its strength. Snipped from the plant and tucked into a pot of compost or glass of water, these plantlets grow away easily. The Spider plant needs moderate light but no direct sun and benefits from being watered with rainwater; however, allow the compost to dry out before watering. If foliage blackens or yellows at the tips, the plant has had too much water.

JADE TREE, MONEY PLANT (*Crassula ovata*): A wonderfully easy plant, the Jade tree needs little water in the summer and even less in the winter. It enjoys full sun, but will tolerate indirect light and only needs feeding once a month in the growing season. Put it outside for the summer and bring it inside before temperatures drop and it will visibly swell and become more vibrant for the experience, casting off any poor treatment through the winter. Mature plants, with chunky trunks have a solid, stately appearance. I lugged a large, neglected *Crassula* from place to place through my student years and it flourished, only to meet its end when I neglectfully left it outside too long at the end of the summer and it was caught by frost.

PAPYRUS (*Cyperus papyrus*): This is the real Papyrus plant, and in the right conditions it will grow to a towering 3 metres (10 ft) with tassels of narrow, feathery leaves held on stiff, erect stems. A meagre 1.5 metres (5 ft) is easily achievable. This is a remarkable, elegant plant, quietly exotic yet incredibly easy to grow. The plant's structure is light and airy, yet imposing and lush. It needs good light and warmth all year round and in warm summers, place it in the garden out of the wind to protect it from damage. It can even be put amongst the marginal plants around a pond while the weather is warm. The root ball should be kept damp at all times, so it is best stood in a saucer of water or a large waterproof vessel with a few centimetres (inches) of water in the bottom. This plant is excellent for those who find regular or careful watering a chore. Feed every couple of weeks in the summer.

UMBRELLA SEDGE (*Cyperus involucratus*) A close relative of true Papyrus, this plant lacks its height and distinction. The leaves clustered at the top of the plant are wider and more grass-like though it enjoys similar conditions. It is one of the easiest plants to propagate – simply cut off one stalk and submerge the bundle of leaves in a glass of water. It will produce roots and shoots and can be potted up to make a new plant.

DRAGON TREE (*Dracaena marginata* and *D. draco*): Commonly used as a houseplant, it has clusters of strap-like leaves with a red edging held on a greyish trunk. It will do well in a bright spot and can be acclimatized to full sun. The plant requires moderate watering and even less in the winter. Feed every two weeks in the growing season. *D. draco* (also commonly known as Dragon Tree) is a native of Tenerife, will tolerate colder temperatures and thrives in full sun. It looks much like a yucca plant. These are reasonably easy plants to keep, and it is normal for their leaves to die at the base of the cluster;

ABOVE *The foliage of the Papyrus plant is very special; its unusual clusters of thread-like leaves held aloft on rigid stalks are uncomplicated but attention-grabbing. Provided the plant has enough water and heat it is delightfully straightforward to grow.*

RIGHT *The Jade tree was one of the first plants I grew as a child and I still grow them now; although they are not amongst the most beautiful plants, they are the most tolerant of neglect. This monster spends the summer outdoors and is hauled inside before the weather gets too cold.*

when this happens simply pull them away. The plants will enjoy occasional misting, though *D. draco* will tolerate less humidity. If possible choose a multi-stemmed Dragon Tree since the colour and texture of the trunk is as much a part of the plant's appeal as its leaves.

RUBBER PLANT (*Ficus elastica*): This is a tough structual plant – in good health it has thick, shiny leaves and grows rapidly with little care. However, it is rather stolid and arguably a little unfashionable, but if you want an easy plant for a dim corner it is a good choice. An interest pot and the right location can add to its appeal. Keep its growing medium just moist, feed infrequently in the growing season, and keep out of direct sunlight (which will scorch the leaves), and the plant should flourish. If the lower leaves become yellow it is either because the plant is pot-bound or more likely it is being over-watered.

ABOVE LEFT *The large-leaved Rubber plant has a solid, dependable look, which matches its character. With just the minimum of care it should be a good, reliable, long-lived plant.*

ABOVE *The creamy margins of the leaves of* Ficus benjamina *'Starlight' are just enough to brighten the foliage but not strident enough to be distracting. It makes a definite contribution to hallways and other awkward spaces.*

WEEPING FIG (*Ficus benjamina*): Far more attractive and a little more difficult than its relative, the Rubber plant, this *Ficus* forms a feathered tree shape with graceful foliage. The most common problem encountered with this plant is getting the watering regime right; it requires little water though enjoys a good level of humidity. Too much water and the leaves turn yellow and drop from the plant. Do not water until the compost is dry for a couple of centimetres (inches) down and mist frequently or stand the plant in a pebble tray. It also dislikes draughts and direct sunlight.

CREEPING FIG (*Ficus pumila*): This climbing plant, most often sold as a houseplant in its variegated form, is easy to keep and requires partial shade. It has small leaves on a jumble of stems. It makes a good subject for the front of a group of plants or as a green groundcover under larger plants.

NERVE PLANT, MOSAIC PLANT (*Fittonia*): A mass of small intricately marked leaves gives this modest-sized plant bags of character and it can come in pinks as well. It will survive in areas with bright or dim indirect light and a constant warm temperature all year round. Water with rainwater, feed once a month or use a slow-release food.

BELOW *The elaborate markings on the leaves of* Fittonia *and the small scale of this neat example, make this one of the prettiest foliage plants.*

IVY (*Hedera*): Incredibly easy to care for and this tough, versatile plant is available in a plethora of leaf sizes and variegations. A general rule of thumb is that those with greener leaves tolerate lower light levels. Large-leaved cultivars look more striking and are best used as large plants, trained up moss poles, while smaller-leaved cultivars are just that bit prettier and are a useful foil for flowering plants. Small-leaved plants, if allowed to grow too extensively, can look a little busy, particularly if they have many-coloured variegation. Keep ivies out of full sun, with moist compost and feed occasionally. It can be cut back to keep it in shape and trained around any kind of wire support.

PINK POLKA DOT PLANT (*Hypoestes phyllostachya*): As its name suggests, the original Polka Dot Plant has deep-green leaves with sweet, perfectly pink spots. Now there are cultivars with different coloured spots and splashes. To keep its striking leaf colour the plant requires bright, indirect light but no direct sun, which will scorch the leaves. It does best when temperatures are around 20°C (68°F) all year round with high humidity. Regular misting is essential to keep this little plant leafy and it will appreciate a feed every couple of weeks in the summer. If the plant begins to get a little straggly nip back the growing tips. This plant is straightforward to keep in a warm bright room.

PEPEROMIA (*Peperomia*): This small tropical plant is often sold in bloom, and although the flowers provide some interest with their white slender spikes held on stiff stalks, they are not especially striking. However, the foliage of this houseplant can be incredibly useful. The plant enjoys good indirect light to partial shade, misting occasionally and watering with soft water once the foliage begins to dry out. Feed only in the summer.

PHILODENDRON (*Philodendron scandens*): Sometimes called the Sweetheart plant because of its heart-shaped leaves, this Philodendron is an easy, lush climber that grows at a good pace. A native of tropical rainforests, it needs good light, humidity and a reasonable temperature all year round. Keep its compost just moist but not waterlogged and feed once a month in spring and summer. This is not a plant for a starring role, but it is a good solid foliage plant that will deliver a punch of fresh green to enhance a lifeless spot.

ALUMINIUM PLANT (*Pilea cadierei*): This small plant makes a valuable contribution as a houseplant because of the bright, silvery patches on its leaves. Growing only 40 cm (16 in) high, it is useful at the front of groupings or when used to under-plant larger specimens with similar requirements. Since it will grow in partial shade, the bright markings on its leaves can be used to lighten a dim corner, though it will grow well in any diffuse light. Keep the compost moist through the summer, water less in the winter, mist occasionally and pick a warm room.

ABOVE *A modestly sized foliage plant, the Aluminium plant's appeal lies in the striking metallic patches daubed on its leaves.*

LEFT *A native of the hedgerow, ivy is incredibly easy to keep, but in a wisely chosen pot and in the right situation it looks as good as any rare and fragile tropical plant.*

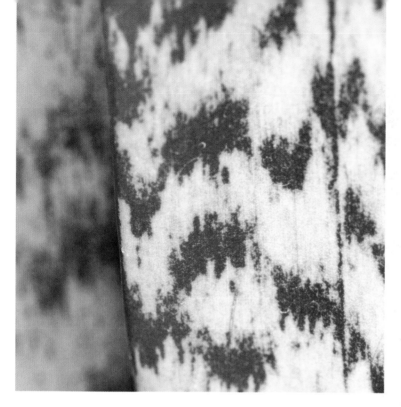

LEFT Sansevieria *has many different forms; this* Sansevieria zeylanica *with dark-green banded leaf markings is less strident than those with yellow leaf margins.*

MOTHER-IN-LAW'S TONGUE (*Sansevieria trifasciata*): A true survivor, ideal for those who have previously failed to keep houseplants for long or those who just do not have the time to nurture a plant. The tall, robust leaves of the *Sansevieria* will reach about 100 cm (39 in) tall and though it is a houseplant with a long tradition, its architectural, unfussy vertical form makes it suited to the most contemporary of interiors. It enjoys bright light but will tolerate much less and only need watering when the compost is completely dry; regular under-watering will not cause a problem. If the leaves flop over or lose rigidity it is a sign that it has been over-watered. Feed just once a month in the growing season.

ARROWHEAD VINE (*Syngonium podophyllum*): This plant is very much like the Philodendron (see page 79) in character – both are climbers with heart-shaped leaves, though the *Syngonium* has the added charm of cultivars with patterned leaves. It needs bright diffuse light though it will tolerate a less well-lit location. It will flourish if the compost is kept moist, is fed regularly in the growing season and the atmosphere is warm and humid.

INCH PLANT (*Tradescantia zebrina* and *T. blossfeldiana*): One of the easiest plants to keep, though not always the most appealing, this trailing plant will grow in any reasonably well-lit spot in hanging baskets, cascading off shelves or tops of tall furniture. It is useful for softening the stark, hard edges of furniture. It needs to be kept moist and fed in the growing season. Green varieties will tolerate lower light levels than the more common variegated cultivars, which have more sparkle.

RIGHT Tradescantia zebrina *has sumptuously coloured foliage with a slightly velvety texture. As a trailing plant it can be used in hanging baskets, or to trail from pots of larger plants hiding the surface of the soil, or to cascade from a mantelpiece.*

Ferns

ABOVE *To keep the foliage of ferns looking green and fresh, make sure they have a good level of humidity.*

Ferns, with their pure, lush green foliage, have a vibrant freshness and their arching fronds bring a feeling of natural purity to a room. However, a tatty, unhappy fern looks dreadful; it is one of those plants that has to be absolutely bursting with health to look good. And seemingly overnight its fortunes can change, its fronds droop a little and the magic is gone. Fortunately, while some ferns are demanding, others are magnificently hearty and will thrive in some of the more difficult spots in the house.

Using the look of the foliage of a plant to assess its constitution works well with ferns. The enticingly flimsy look of the Maidenhair fern is indicative of the plant's delicate constitution, and without a constant high level of humidity the plant quickly shrivels. Once the Maidenhair fern wilts, it cannot be resurrected; unlike other wilting houseplants miraculously restored by a good soaking this one cannot be restored by such treatment. If the plant does dry out and the foliage droops irrevocably it is worth trimming away the dead foliage, restoring good humidity and watering regularly as new shoots may appear. The glossy leaves of the Bird's Nest fern and Fishtail fern look more robust and they are.

Though it might be natural to associate ferns with damp, cool woodlands, most ferns used as houseplants hale from tropical climes and so require more warmth than one might expect to keep them happy. Most ferns will prefer a daytime temperature of 18.5–24°C (65–75°F) and a temperature of 13°C (55°F) at night. Some may favour even higher temperatures, but as they are mainly forest floor dwellers, none can tolerate direct sunlight, and their green fronds are quickly scorched to a crisp brown. Ferns are the perfect choice for spots where there is insufficient light for most other plants. They are happiest on north-facing windowsills and the filtered light of screened windows and east-facing windows in the winter. They will grow happily where there is a reasonable level of indirect light.

High humidity is vital to keep fern fronds looking fresh. Most would prefer at least 30–50 percent humidity (most homes are kept at below 10 percent), making them a good choice for the bathroom where steam from baths and showers helps to keep the air moist. The poor light in most bathrooms created by small, shaded or obscured glass will suit them, too. Elsewhere a mulch of sphagnum moss on the surface of the pot, misting with water at room temperature and sitting the pot in a pebble tray filled with water will help stoke up the humidity around the plant. However, the pots should never be sat in the water of the pebble tray or the roots will rot. Grouping ferns with other plants will help maintain humidity. On the following pages are some easy-going ferns that are less exacting and tolerate less-than-perfect care; choose one of these if you want an easy option.

ABOVE *Unlike the verdant lush woodland ferns, the Staghorn fern is an epiphyte and will be quite at home more or less hung from the wall.*

Easy ferns

BOSTON FERN (*Nephrolepis exaltata* 'Bostoniensis'): Forming a tousled dome of fronds, this fern is not the most elegant plant but if kept in good order it looks very striking. There are a variety of cultivars available with slight variations on the basic divided frond shape. The Boston Fern has been a popular choice for a houseplant since the 19th century and when displayed in a period jardinière on a pedestal it has a Victorian or country house charm. These ferns are very long-lived and the mass of fronds will gradually expand.

BIRD'S NEST FERN (*Asplenium nidus*): The undivided, bright green fronds of the Bird's Nest fern form a cone, with new fronds uncurling from tightly spiralled ammonites at the centre of the plant. This is a very neat plant with a strong form, unlike the sprawling Boston fern. Its shining, bright leaves and orderly habit suit it to many decorative styles, even the most contemporary. Small subjects look wonderful in a linear group of three thanks to their architectural form. Even fully grown, a Bird's Nest fern will probably only reach 50–60 cm (20–24 in).

HOLLY FERN (*Cyrtomium falcatum* 'Rochfordianum') or **FISHTAIL FERN** (*C. falcatum*): The fronds of these robust ferns have the appearance of holly leaves arranged along a tough, wiry stalk. The fronds are lime-green when new, maturing to a deep, glossy green. It will tolerate temperatures of -5–30°C (23–86°F) more light and a drier atmosphere than some ferns. Once again this is a potted plant with a long history, and was commonplace in the 19th century.

STAGHORN FERN (*Platycerium*): If you want a curiosity, a real statement, then choose a Staghorn fern. Though it needs particular growing conditions once those are in place, this majestic fern is not hard to keep. It is probably best kept in a bathroom as it does need a humid atmosphere. This fern does not grow in soil, but the fronds, which resemble deer antlers (if you squint a bit), grow from a shield that is simply attached to a piece of bark with some sphagnum moss. To look 'right' these ferns need to be attached to walls or hung from the ceiling. Normally they are sold in some kind of hanging basket. Watering is slightly arduous as the plant must be removed from where it hangs and the shield of the plant must be submerged in lukewarm water.

Bromeliads and Air plants

ABOVE *The colourful flower structures of Guzmanias will last for months; however, like some other bromeliads, the plant may die after flowering. It should leave a host of pups or offsets that you can pot up.*

Tropical and tolerant, the bromeliads look incredibly exotic but are remarkably straightforward to care for, and one group of bromeliads, known as Air plants, need no compost at all. Most bromeliads have leaves that form a vase or funnel giving them a striking, rigid form suited to contemporary interiors. Their foliage can be interestingly coloured, while intensely coloured inflorescences and bracts around relatively insignificant flowers give a concentrated shot of improbable, bold colour.

Most frequently, bromeliads are offered for sale in flower because this is when they have most impact and their eye-catching inflorescences will last for a few weeks or even months. Knowing many bromeliads will only flower once can save a great deal of effort in trying to make them flower again. Not only that, most will die within a year or two of flowering. Before it dies, the plant should produce small plantlets around its base, which can be removed and potted up, but the safest and easiest option is to leave them to grow as a cluster. These small plants, often referred to as 'pups' may then flower when mature. To encourage flowering, place a plant in a location where it will receive a good dose of bright light. Stand a fruit bowl nearby can help as ripening bananas produce the gas ethylene, which may stimulate flowering.

Despite hailing from the tropics, these plants are very easy to keep, withstanding a range of temperatures and light levels. Most are happiest in bright, indirect sunlight, though *Vriesea* bromeliads (of which there are 250 species and many hybrids) in particular will adapt to low light levels. Most bromeliads will survive temperatures close to freezing and up to 38°C (100°F), though they will do best in a steady 15.5–32°C (60–90°F) daytime temperature. Bromeliads that form a funnel or vase with their foliage are known as funnel or tank bromeliads, the funnel at the base of the leaves should always contain water and the plants should be watered and fed by topping up this reservoir. Every now and again the funnel should be emptied of water and fresh water added, since the plants absorb water and nutrients through their leaves. The compost in the pot need only be watered when dry. Most bromeliads thrive in a humid atmosphere, so providing a pebble tray is a good idea. Feeding with a liquid fertilizer once a month in the growing season should be sufficient and for funnel bromeliads pour straight into the funnel.

As many bromeliads are epiphytes (plants that naturally live on trees) their roots are purely to anchor them, so large plants can be housed in surprisingly small containers. If a plant does require a larger pot it is best planted in a 50/50 mix of orchid compost and soil-less or loam-free compost.

ABOVE *Keep the funnel of this type of bromeliad topped up with water. Every now and again, flush out the funnel by watering the plant until it overflows; this will prevent the water from becoming stagnant.*

Brilliant bromeliads

AECHMEA (*Aechmea*): This epiphytic funnel bromeliad forms very colourful bracts that will last for months. It thrives in bright light. Sadly, however, it is one of those plants that may die after flowering, hopefully leaving 'pups'. Simply remove the dead rosettes.

QUEEN'S TEARS, FRIENDSHIP PLANT (*Billbergia nutans*): This vase-shaped bromeliad will tolerate bright light to slight shade. Flowering in spring, this plant is very easy to keep. The showy pink bracts surrounding its flowers will last for several weeks. When not in bloom its glossy strap-like leaves mean it is

The flowering structures of bromeliads are sensationally colourful and add an exotic splash to interior decorative schemes.

RIGHT *Spectacular and otherworldly, this hearty-looking Aechmea set in a rustic basket and mulched with moss, will probably carry this inflorescence for months.*

still attractive enough to earn its keep. A native of tropical South America it will enjoy plenty of water in the summer and less in the winter.

EARTH STAR (*Cryptanthus*): Commonly named 'Earth Stars', these bromeliads are incredibly easy to keep and unlike some others that rely on flashy bracts for their charm, these plants have handsome rosettes of foliage with slightly waved edges. The cultivar most often available has attractively striped leaves, while the white flowers it produces are pretty but unimportant. It grows best in indirect light and like many of the other plants in this group it is naturally a terrestrial plant (growing in soil, so the compost needs to be watered regularly, but allowed to dry a little in between.

DYCKIA (*Dyckia*): As desert natives the spiny-leaved plants in this group will tolerate the brightest locations and little or slightly negligent watering. The spines on the leaves are ferocious so place it with care, especially if there are young children in the house. They are able to survive long periods without water by becoming dormant. The plants vary considerably but all bear multiple blooms from the side of the plant if they get enough sunshine.

GUZMANIA (*Guzmania*): Grown for their outstandingly colourful flower bracts, the Guzmanias are less able to adapt to bright light than other bromeliads and should not be subjected to direct sunlight. They have a rosette of dark leaves that grow to a greater height than many bromeliads. Like a number of other bromeliads, they form a funnel or tank with their foliage and should be watered into that funnel.

NEOREGELIA (*Neoregelia*): The draw of this group of bromeliads is the new leaves, which are flushed from pale pink and to glossy pillar-box red. They need good light levels to achieve intense colours and some claim that feeding actually reduces the colouration.

FLAMING SWORD PLANT (*Vriesea splendens*): The flat, tall, brilliant red flowering part of the most commonly sold *Vriesea* gives it its common name. These startling structures will last for months, and when they finally fade, carefully cut them away at the base as *Vriesea* carries its young plants or 'pups' in its vase or tank rather than around the outside. Like all tank or funnel bromeliads it should be watered into its central cup and requires very weak liquid fertilizer in the growing season. It prefers indirect light, but will acclimatize to direct light.

Air plants

One group of bromeliads, known as Air plants, need no compost at all. The genus *Tillandsia* is an extraordinary-looking group of plants that are one of the easiest to care for once you know how it is done. It is also a slightly abused group of plants; though they can look stunning treated in the right way, they are often sold glued to inappropriate ornaments. As they require no soil these little plants can be grown on just about anything; they need not be permanently attached, and in fact it is best if they can be easily removed for watering, though they can be tied with nylon ties if required and if absolutely necessary secured with water-based, non-toxic glue. Arranged in modern glass vessels they look chic while resting on tactile pieces of driftwood they have an earthy, natural appeal. These elegant plants are wonderful for those who enjoy change, for though the plants themselves are almost unchanging, they can be arranged and rearranged into a myriad of displays. These plants are best purchased from specialist suppliers on the Internet or at horticultural shows, free from any plastic trappings.

Often flagged up as a plant for those who cannot keep anything else alive, Air plants are easy to maintain. They tolerate bright light, a great range of temperatures, will withstand under-watering and are impossible to over-water. Though misting is recommended, swishing the plants in soft water or rainwater is the best way to hydrate them. Just dip them into a bowl of water, move around gently and shake off any excess water. If you want to feed the plant, add some very dilute liquid feed to the bowl. That is it! If the leaves of the plant curl inwards along their length then they are too dry and can be left in the water for half an hour or so.

LEFT *If Air plants are not glued to a support they can be watered by swishing them in a bowl of tepid water and then shaking off the excess.*

BELOW *Vibrant Air plants make an interesting wall display.*

BELOW RIGHT *Three small Air plants poked into the hollows of a piece of weathered driftwood create an unusual display in front of three grouped terracotta pots of* Aeonium arboreum *'Schwarzkopf'.*

Bonsai

Bonsai trees are special; they evoke strong opinions, and the gnarled, aged look either appeals to you or you just see tortured, stunted, deformed plants. The ancient art produces miniature trees with an abundance of character and immediately recognizable Oriental charm. Though forming bonsai and caring for very old specimens is best left to the enthusiast, there are some inexpensive specimens that will thrive with a little care and still imbue a room that special character of Oriental elegance and restraint.

Many bonsai are not suited as houseplants and prefer to spend the greater part of the year outside. Trees that are native to tropical, subtropical and Mediterranean regions will do well inside, though even these plants will benefit from a spell outdoors in a sheltered spot when the weather is favourable. As the plants are in such small amounts of compost in shallow pans it is important to keep conditions as favourable as possible; unfortunately, it is easy to both under- and over-water. The results of under-watering quickly become obvious as the plant wilts, and for the most part this can be rectified quickly by effective watering. The damage caused by over-watering takes longer to show – leaves become yellow and fall from the tree and roots rot away. The Japanese say it takes three years to learn how to water bonsai properly, so I almost feel embarrassed to offer these few words of advice. Do not try to impose a watering routine, rather, check the compost daily and only water when the top half-inch has dried out. Assess this by gently poking a pencil or your finger into the compost at the edge of the pan and check how damp it appears.

Pruning need not be difficult. If you buy a pleasingly shaped tree simply keep cutting it back to that framework. If you wish to improve the shape, cut away growth accordingly. The trees cannot be left without pruning but equally there is no need to primp your tree daily, just look at it every now and again. Use sharp scissors or secateurs to cleanly snip away growth.

Pot on your bonsai tree in the spring – every year or every two years for larger trees – and always into a shallow bonsai pan just a little larger than the last. When you move plants to a new container, trim any straggling roots and use a growing medium designed for bonsai.

Bonsai are serious houseplants; they are unmistakeably refined and dignified, the kind of plant that sits well on an antique desk or used as a focal point in a pared-down interior. The older a tree the more expensive it is likely to be; there are tricks, however, to give the impression of great age so if you wish to invest in a truly remarkable bonsai go to a reputable nursery and get plenty of advice on caring for that particular tree.

BONSAI FOR GROWING INDOORS

- Azalea
- Gardenia
- Indian hawthorn
- Umbrella tree
- Banyan fig
- Weeping fig
- Pomegranate

RIGHT *It is wise to put your dedication to the test with a small, relatively inexpensive indoor bonsai before purchasing a more expensive specimen. Allowing a tree that has absorbed 50 or even 100 years of the bonsai grower's art to perish through lack of care is a little more serious than letting a primrose die.*

Cacti and succulents

Adapted to live in challenging conditions, these plants make tough, reliable and easy-to-keep houseplants, ideal for those who have little time to devote to houseplants or who must spend long stretches of time away from home. The term 'succulent' applies to plants suited to growing in dry conditions; they have structures designed to store water and keep moisture loss to a minimum. Technically, cacti are succulents whose leaves have become spines and the stem takes over the functions normally carried out by leaves.

Though cacti and succulents can bear outstanding blooms, they are usually grown for their interesting and geometric forms that sit particularly well in modern, clean-lined interiors where more lush plants may look out of place. While many of the plants have an alluring geometric perfection or flawless shape, some are rather ungainly and unattractive; the Prickly Pear and even the popular Christmas cactus, for example, can become straggly. There are also strange cacti that look like the work of Dr Frankenstein, where sections of stems from two plants are grafted together, presumably just because it is possible, but to me these plants look uncomfortably odd. These oddities and small spiky cacti in tiny pots often appeal to children, and once they understand to avoid touching the spines these make excellent plants for children to collect.

There are hundreds of cacti and succulents available and their exact requirements will vary; if you want the startling flowers some cacti produce it may take some patience and manipulation of temperatures, but that aside they survive with the bare minimum of care.

ABOVE *Tiny cacti are often the first plants children are given to grow; these are a good choice so long as the children learn to respect the spines. Even those that appear fluffy have needle-sharp spines.*

RIGHT *Multiplying by three gives more impact to the combination of simple sunshine yellow pots and inexpensive cacti.*

Desert and forest cacti

Desert cacti are those with pads, domes and candelabra forms. They need very little water except in spring and summer when they can be watered occasionally and the compost allowed to almost completely dry out before watering again. Desert cacti require plenty of light and will tolerate direct sunlight. In the winter subjecting them to lower temperatures will help encourage flowering. Deserts are scorching hot in the day but temperatures drop at night so cacti will tolerate lower temperatures than expected.

Forest cacti, on the other hand, have flattened stems like a series of leaves strung together; the most commonly grown varieties of forest cacti need slightly different care from desert cacti, especially since their main appeal lies in the lavish eruption of blooms produced each year (Christmas cacti belong in this group). Triggering this blossoming requires a series of temperature

Fabulous foliage

changes and regulation of water supply. To stimulate blooming the plants must have a dormant period of cool with little water, normally sometime in autumn and winter, followed by a period of heat and plenty of water. They can spend summers outside if the weather is hospitable.

Succulents

There are literally hundreds of species of succulents in existence and the adaptation to arid climates has resulted in some beautiful and almost indestructible plants. Because the group is so diverse and the shapes so varied, there is bound to be a succulent to fit most interior styles and conditions. All succulents enjoy good light, though direct sunlight through a window may scorch some succulents. Too little light and plants can become stretched and 'leggy'. Allow the compost to dry out between watering and reduce the amount of water given to almost nothing in the winter. Over-watering results in soft, pulpy foliage and root rot.

LEFT *Many succulent plants like this Echeveria have a delicate, dusty kind of 'bloom' on their leaves; touching it or careless watering produces green spots or smudges and spoils the effect. Warmth and light are crucial for this easy houseplant, which normally needs no encouragement to throw up flower spikes.*

RIGHT *This unusual treatment really shows off the succulent to good effect, the greens of the layers of sand echoing the colours of the plant. The mulch used around succulents is not only effective in showing off the plant, it also helps protect the plant from a build-up of damp around the base of the stem that might result in the plant rotting.*

Palms and cycads

Redolent of beaches, exotic oases and tropical verdure, palms are a versatile group of plants, many of which are amongst the least demanding and most forgiving plants you can choose to grow indoors. Perhaps their popularity as houseplants comes from this tolerance of poor conditions shared by many species coupled with the unmistakeable air of luxurious splendour that a healthy palm brings to a room. Extravagant green fronds create the elegant forms and strong silhouettes desirable in indoor plants.

Although most palms sold as houseplants hail from tropical climates, average room temperature is adequate and many will tolerate low light levels and irregular watering. Not all palms are this forgiving. Most are slow growing and long-lived. Having a lustrous-looking palm starts with choosing a healthy specimen in the nursery or garden centre. Like all plants, reject any plant that has browning leaves or any sign of pests or disease (see pages 128–30); however, do not be too concerned if roots are growing from the drainage holes in the pot. Many palms enjoy being pot-bound, and in fact some experts say these should not be repotted until they literally break out of the pot. The other aspect to look out for when choosing a palm is whether it has been forced to grow tall very quickly by controlling the light it receives. Taller plants look more impressive and will sell well, so it makes sense for nurseries to encourage palms to grow upwards quickly by reducing light levels; however, this weakens plants and makes them less robust.

Common palm problems

BROWN LEAVES: Lower leaves or fronds die naturally as they are replaced by new larger fronds. Remove the brown leaves to keep the plant looking tidy and to reduce the risk of disease.

BROWN LEAF TIPS: Often seemingly healthy palms will get brown, crispy leaf tips that spoil the look of the plant. This is a sign that the plant has gone short of water or humidity or got too cold. Snip off the brown tips to improve the look of the plant.

BROWN PATCHES OR SPOTS ON LEAVES: This is probably the result of a virus encouraged by over-watering. Allow the compost to dry a little between watering and ensure that the plant is not sitting in water. Remove all the affected leaves to improve.

YELLOW LEAVES: These are a sign that the plant is starving and needs feeding. Use a palm fertilizer in line with the manufacturer's instructions.

ABOVE *Though it will eventually reach about 1 metre (10 ft) high, the tough Parlour palm is one of the most graceful palms even when small.*

FAR RIGHT *The strong form and deep green of the Sago palm works well amongst the gleam of this metallic group of objects. The Sago is in fact a cycad, which evolved millions of years ago before flowering plants appeared.*

Easy palms

KENTIA PALM (*Howea forsteriana*): This is a tough palm, so do not be fooled by the grace of its gently bending pinnate fronds that make it look like a prima donna – it will put up with a great deal. A Kentia palm will survive in the dullest corners, though it would prefer bright indirect light; it can also adapt to full sun. Water with rainwater when the compost begins to dry out and when you need to pot on, use an ericaceous compost.

SAGO PALM (*Cycas revoluta*): The Sago palm has survived since dinosaurs roamed the earth and was much loved by the Victorians as a houseplant. It lacks a little of the refined character of many palms as its leaves are far stiffer and a darker green with symmetrically placed needle-like projections. It has a solid, architectural shape that suits masculine or modern decorative styles. It enjoys a well-lit spot but not direct sunlight. Occasional misting will be most welcome and it only needs watering when the compost dries out.

PARLOUR PALM (*Chamaedorea elegans*): This palm will grow in just about any room with a reasonable amount of indirect light. It does require a good level of humidity and regular watering, particularly if temperatures are high; the leaves are quick to develop brown tips if these are lacking. This is a palm from the jungle and so it enjoys moist humid conditions making it a great choice for the bathroom. A shortage of water will also make the plant more susceptible to red spider mite.

LADY PALM (*Rhapis excelsa*): This palm will tolerate drought and reasonably low light, and enjoys its roots being tightly packed in its pot. This is one of the plants highly recommended as a 'fresh air' plant as it is efficient at removing pollutants from the air (see opposite page).

BUTTERFLY PALM (*Chrysalidocarpus lutescens*): The Butterfly (or Areca) palm needs a steady warm temperature all year round – anything less than 18°C (65°F) will cause its leaves to yellow. Despite its need for warmth, it cannot tolerate direct light but will do best in bright, indirect light. Its compost should be kept moist at all times and frequent misting will help keep this palm looking lush.

Palms to avoid

COCONUT PALM (*Cocos nucifera*): Seductively tall with rigid fronds growing straight from a large nut on the surface of the compost, these plants are appealing because they look impressive but cost relatively little. This is because they grow quickly and a 1.8 metre (6 ft) specimen is still just a baby; however, they are very hard to keep. If you accept they will be short-lived and you just want a wonderfully statuesque plant for a short time then go ahead.

ABOVE *The Butterfly palm needs a good level of humidity. If the air around it is too dry it can suffer from spider mites and its leaves quickly brown at the tips.*

Fresh-air plants

Not only do houseplants have a genuinely beneficial psychological effect on people according to some scientific studies, further research has shown that plants can make our homes healthier places to live in by removing chemicals from the air. In a nutshell, plants can clean up indoor air pollution and chemicals released in our homes. As we strive to regulate the temperature in our homes they may suffer from lack of fresh air circulation and volatile organic chemicals can build up. Through their leaves, plants absorb chemicals such as formaldehyde, acetone, methyl alcohol, ethyl acetate and ammonia, which can be released from furnishings and building materials, and also bio-effluent (released by people). Once absorbed, the chemicals are moved to the roots of the plants where the plants processes them or microbes in the soil break them down. Plants also take in the polluted air within the house and pump out oxygen.

All plants will remove chemicals to some degree but detailed research (some by NASA), has determined which plants are particularly good at cleaning up the air in our homes and even which particular chemicals each plant might excel in mopping up. (See a fascinating book by Dr B. C. Wolverton entitled *How to Grow Fresh Air*, for detailed information). Plants can be beneficial everywhere in the home, but it makes sense to place fresh-air plants where you spend a great deal of time, relaxing or at a computer screen.

EASY AND EFFECTIVE FRESH-AIR PLANTS

- Kentia palm
- Lady palm
- Swiss Cheese plant
- Philodendron
- Miniature Date palm
- Peace lily
- Corn plant
- Boston fern
- Rubber plant

RIGHT *With enormously decorative fan-shaped fronds, the Lady palm will not only do well in a poorly lit area, it is renowned as an effective fresh-air plant.*

Containers

Whether it is a stylish prop that allows an unexceptional plant to take centre stage or the subtle foil that shows off a spectacular plant to its very best advantage – container selection is just as important as the choice of plant. The way you chose to combine pot and plant will subtly alter the character of both. Choosing a simple container makes the plant the star, and a humble plant in a lavish or ornate vessel reverses the balance. It is not just the style or character that makes this partnership successful, the container needs to work with the scale of the plant too. A large plant will reasonably require a large container, not just for visual balance but as plants become taller and heavier, a weighty container can help to keep them stable. However, playing with scale can have some very stylish results, a large container furnished with just a single, simple succulent or Spider plant can look striking.

The basics

ABOVE *Junk shop finds like this wonderfully worn wooden box provide the opportunity to create a display that is totally unique. It makes a fantastic home for pots of basil and parsley.*

Every houseplant you buy will come with a pot, but sadly, these need to be disguised by cachepots for two reasons. Firstly, they are usually very unattractive plastic flowerpots and secondly, their drainage holes allow water to seep from the bottom of the pot. For this reason, the easiest containers to use are watertight. Lining porous containers or baskets with stout polythene is possible, but there is always the risk that the polythene lining may be damaged and furniture ruined as you water. Some seemingly watertight ceramics may not be if not completely glazed inside and out.

As they sit on polished surfaces, damp seeps from the base leaving a nasty ring only to be revealed when you move the plant.

Though you may buy a particular cachepot for a particular plant, the reality is that for most of us, the cachepot will probably see many plant occupants over the years. They are the durable part of the partnership and as such should be seen as a solid investment. Building up a stock of useful containers makes sense, especially if you intend to use plenty of transient seasonal plants and bulbs. There are plenty of options, and you don't have to spend a fortune; junk shops, your kitchen cupboards, and possibly even the recycling bin will harbour lots of useful pots and containers. Plastic boxes, vases, watering cans, tin cans, mugs, jugs, basins, colanders, baskets, glasses, soup tureens, biscuit tins and jars will all work well with the right plant in the right setting. Finding a quirky, unexpected container can introduce a real sense of fun.

BELOW *Reflective metallic containers always brighten a space – even in a dull corner they will reflect and radiate light. Most will suit a contemporary decorative scheme.*

Quick cover-ups

Quick and easy cover transformations to seasonal potted plants provide the perfect answer to the need for table decorations, party plants and those seasonal flowering plants that will be with you for just a few weeks. There are a number of transformation options, including using pretty gift bags or boxes, scraps of fabric, ribbons and wrapping paper. Depending on the plants and the wrapping you choose, the results can be colourful, pretty, quirky or sophisticated as the setting demands. The only drawback of these nifty transformations is that the disguises employed are unlikely to be waterproof. If the plant is simply sat in a gift bag or box, it can easily be removed for watering, while a polythene bag can be hidden under the paper or fabric.

ABOVE LEFT *The quickest container of all – gift or party bags make a quirky, inexpensive cover-up for this pretty miniature rose.*

ABOVE *A colourful wrap can give an ordinary plant more character; a pretty lavender gingham tied wth a narrow matching ribbon is the perfect wrap for a fragrant pot of lavender.*

Mulch

Interesting mulch over the surface of the compost of a houseplant is a wonderful final addition, adding another element of texture and colour to the display. Serving more than just an ornamental purpose, a decorative layer of mulch applied over the surface of the soil of a houseplant has the practical advantage of reducing the rate that water evaporates from the compost. In the case of many succulents, the mulch provides a foil to show off the plant, giving the plant more presence than it would possess against the dark soil. Other upright plants leave an expanse of bare soil that simply looks better when disguised. The right mulch can liven up a so-so plant or group of plants or provide the link that unites pot and plant. There are no hard-and-fast rules about what to use to dress the soil. Ferns will enjoy a blanket of fluffy, fresh green moss, but in most situations, it will be unimportant whether you choose glass beads, shells, buttons or fir cones. Garden centres are increasingly stocking a range of products specifically produced to cover the soil of potted plants but these can be expensive and there is no reason why you should not improvise with anything from the corks from wine bottles to marbles.

BELOW *Chunky, tactile pebbles make practical, natural mulch for larger plants; they can be salvaged, washed and used repeatedly.*

BELOW RIGHT *Crisp, ice-like shards of recycled glass throw these succulents into sharp relief; against the bare soil their interesting shapes would be much less obvious. Glass products are available in many different colours so there is plenty of scope for creativity.*

The right spot

The effect a plant has on the way a room looks, its mood and its style, is easy to see; observing if the plant has what it needs to thrive is much harder. It is possible to generalize about the character of different rooms in any house: kitchens and bathrooms are humid and may have low light levels; main sitting and drawing rooms are, as a rule, bright and the most consistently heated rooms; halls and landings tend to be poorly lit and draughty. Plants are often flagged up for these standardized situations accordingly, but all homes are different, so the only way to decide what conditions are like in a certain room or location in your home is to pause and take time to assess them.

Great survivors

Your plant will be sensitive to light, humidity, heat and draughts. There are certain situations that are better avoided – near radiators, fireplaces and badly insulated doors and windows. Where the conditions are extreme – windowsills in full sun, extreme heat, an arid atmosphere and very low light levels – very few plants will survive. Cold draughts and extreme temperature fluctuations are also challenging. There are, however, plants that will positively revel in these extremes and others that will do well enough to look good, when all else fails. These 'survivor' plants are as tough as the proverbial old boots and will not only survive a poor location, but also poor care. So if all else fails, try a plant from our 'survivor' list (right). Though I should add hastily, they are not everlasting and will die if completely abandoned; and obviously they will look perkier when well cared for.

A FEW GREAT SURVIVORS

- Cast-iron plant
- Ponytail palm
- Spider plant
- Jade plant
- Haworthia
- Ivy
- Pothos
- Mother-in-law's Tongue
- Arrowhead plant

LEFT *Needing little water or food, and tolerating long periods of drought, this well-placed Ponytail palm is a fantastic survivor.*

Difficult conditions

Hot spots and sun-lovers

In the summer, there are just a few real sun-lovers that will stand the baking they are likely to receive through the glass of a south-facing window. In winter, as the sun loses its intensity, more plants will be happy in this spot, particularly those that flower in this season. Cacti and most succulents are the obvious choice for any hot spot; they are equipped to cope with both heat and dry (see box left for some other plants that can take the heat).

Draughty, chilly spots

Many houses have a hall, landing, room or porch that is prone to draughts from outside doors and is often cooler than the rest of the house, especially in older properties. These bleaker areas can really benefit from the uplifting shot of green a potted plant brings. Many plants are particularly intolerant of cold, drying draughts and as many houseplants are natives of tropical or subtropical regions, these situations can be tricky. However, you might try tough plants normally associated with the garden in temperate areas, or use plants that are short-lived in the normal course of events, such as bulbs. Imagine how warming a bowl of flaming orange tulips might be in a chilly corner. The following are some other suggestions.

JAPANESE ARALIA (*Fatsia japonica*): This hardy plant is more often found in the garden but its large, glossy leaves and tropical good looks make it a good choice for cold spots indoors.

COMMON IVY (*Hedera helix*): A real survivor, ivy will do well even in areas where it is regularly blasted with cold air from opening doors. There is a plethora of pretty variagations to choose from.

TREE IVY: An inter-generic hybrid of the two plants above (*Fatsia japonica* and *Hedera helix*), it has the perfect pedigree for a plant to survive a chilly dark corner. It grows into a robust vine with large glossy leaves and a lush, tropical character.

CAST-IRON PLANT (*Aspidistra elatior*): This stalwart with its elegant elongated leaves will survive, but it will look better in a less hostile spot.

BOSTON FERN (*Nephrolepsis exaltata*): If moisture levels are well controlled this stout fern is worth a try.

ABOVE *Most cacti will thrive in a hot spot exposed to the sun. As well as being sun-lovers, these tiny plants are also great survivors.*

SUN-LOVERS
• Phoenix palm
• Cycads
• European Fan palm
• Ponytail palm
• Pelargoniums
• Strelitzia
• Yuccas
• Cacti

Low light

In badly lit interiors, the freshness and colour of potted plants can be a useful tool in brightening the gloom. Though hallways and landings are most prone to low light levels, it can also be a problem in any room in the house with north-facing windows or windows that are heavily shaded. Even in a reasonably bright room, the light can become dim away from the window and in nooks and crannies. Plants suffering from a lack of light become 'leggy' and weak; however, there are plenty of plants that will tolerate the lack of light so team them with a reflective or pale-coloured container to cheer up a shadowy interior. Ferns are an obvious choice and the Boston fern deserves special mention for its tenacity though not for its elegance.

GRAPE IVY (*Cissus rhombifolia*): A vigorous twining climber with prettily cut leaves that will climb or trail depending on the space you would like it to occupy. Keep moderately moist and feed weekly in the summer.

CREEPING FIG (*Ficus pumila*): Unlike its close relatives, the Creeping Fig is a climber that covers entire buildings in its native habitat. The creamy-edged leaves work particularly well in brightening dingy corners.

KENTIA PALM (*Howea forsteriana*): This statuesque palm always looks elegant and tolerates low light levels.

DRAGON TREE (*Dracaena deremensis*): Though it will tolerate low light, the Dragon Tree will also tolerate great heat.

SWEETHEART PLANT (*Philodendron scandens*): Great for a north-facing room, this plant will put up with cool temperatures as well as low light levels.

CAST-IRON PLANT (*Aspidistra elatior*): This tough plant will survive in quite a number of challenging locations.

ABOVE LEFT *Despite its glossy, tropical appearance, this fatsia is as tough as anything. It will bring a little bit of joy to the gloomiest corner.*

ABOVE *The vigorous, small-leaved Creeping fig will tolerate low light levels, and will either climb or trail, depending on how it is trained.*

FAR RIGHT *Poinsettias are excellent plants for a warm and bright spot.*

Plants for bright places

Not all locations are so challenging that they require plants to cope with extremes – in fact most interiors offer situations that will suit a myriad of plants without the plants having to struggle for survival.

A spot with bright indirect light is the easiest location to deal with, as most plants are likely to be happiest in these circumstances, away from direct sunlight but not in heavy shade. It is worth distinguishing between a brightly lit warm room and a well-lit cooler room, since the plants that will flourish in each are slightly different.

Warm and bright

Rooms with large east- and west-facing windows will have good light for a large portion of the day. The middle or edges of a room with south-facing windows will also probably offer the same conditions. Because these are favourable conditions for many plants, you will have lots to chose from; the box (left) will give you some ideas.

Cool and bright

An interior lit by a large north-facing window may be light and bright but it will not benefit from any direct sunlight. Bright cool rooms can be the ideal location for flowering plants; blooms fade more quickly in the warm rooms, in the cool they will last for days longer. Again, these are conditions that many plants favour so you should find something to suit your taste and decor.

WARM AND BRIGHT

- Begonias
- Caladium
- Camellia
- Cape Primrose
- Gardenia
- Gerbera
- Hibiscus
- Christmas cactus
- Jasmine
- Poinsettia
- Aluminium plant
- Papyrus
- Peace Lily

COOL AND BRIGHT

- Clivia
- Azalea
- Bellflowers
- Cyclamen
- Narcissus
- Primula
- Hydrangea
- Moth orchid
- Lilies

Plants room by room

ABOVE *White-flowered amaryllis look wonderfully sophisticated illuminated by candlelight.*

Style and mood, as well as the needs of the plant are important when selecting plants, but the function of the room will lend itself to choosing and using plants in a particular way, with a display tailored to how the room is used.

Entrance halls and landings

Though they may be cool, dim, draughty and cramped, the entrance hall is the place to make a real statement. This is the first room visitors see, the hub of the house through which you probably pass numerous times a day as you move around, though you may not linger. Something showy and eye-catching is in order for this space. A bowl crammed with spring bulbs is ideal, a splash of vibrant colour provided by short-lived flowering bulbs that can be relocated to the garden once spent. Follow these with primroses, pansies or violas – inexpensive plants used en masse to create a stir. Alternatively use a rugged, easy-going plant such as a Boston fern and set it in an outstanding container.

In some entrance halls a certain formality is successful, so you might use carefully clipped topiary shapes to flank the front door outside, which can be mirrored inside, though these plants will need regular restorative holidays outdoors to survive and look healthy.

BELOW *The staircase can make an interesting place to display fairly large plants like this Weeping fig, if there is space and it will not cause a hazard.*

RIGHT *The most tolerant of plants, Mother-in-law's Tongue will survive being put in the corner; here its reflective container adds an extra dash of brightness.*

Sitting room

For the most part, the sitting room is where leisure time is spent; many people invest a great deal in making this a comfortable, attractive space, carefully selecting furniture, soft furnishings and ornaments to create a room in the style they desire. Plants can play a huge part in this process, no matter what type of interior decoration is required. One large specimen or group of plants will add texture and life. The psychological and heath-giving benefits of potted plants are probably most effective here and in the work or office environment. As a rule, sitting rooms will have reasonable-sized window and therefore good light. This room tends to be kept warmer than other parts of the house and so is less humid, so if using plants that require good humidity, stand them in a pebble tray, ensuring though, that the base of the pot is above the water level.

BELOW *Ranged along this simple side table, a combination of Mind-your-own-business,* Kalanchoe *'Magic Bells' and cut flowers provide a refreshing display. The panelled mirror boosts the volume of both plants and light.*

Kitchen

ABOVE *This zingy variegated thyme and its lime-green pot make the perfect couple. Place it on the main worktop where it is within easy snipping reach of the cook.*

ABOVE RIGHT *A number of small herb plants can be crammed into one larger container so the cook can supply snippets to flavour meals over many weeks. Regular picking keeps herbs looking bushy and compact.*

Though most leisure time is spent in the sitting room, most family activity takes place in the kitchen. As the kitchen is usually bright and humid, it is a good location for plants if space allows. In fact, the kitchen windowsill is traditionally the nursery for the plant enthusiast, where cuttings and seedlings are nurtured. For the rest of us, herbs and cut-and-come-again salad leaves make sensible plants for the kitchen, along with aloe to soothe burns and a cheery seasonal display at the centre of the table. Containers taken directly from the kitchen cupboards add a touch of wit, and mixing bowls, jugs and colanders stuffed with plants will look at home in the kitchen. The normal paraphernalia of most kitchens with their bright lights, hard surfaces and fitted cupboards, can make them rather harsh, severe places; plants can help to soften stark lines and make them more comfortable places to be. In a slick contemporary kitchen where such starkness is the intention, neat little succulents in restrained containers or herbs in a sharp stainless steel trough would be appropriate.

Bedroom

Whether you favour minimalist modern furnishings, romantic chintz or the glowing patina of furniture evoking country-house charm, most of us aspire to create a tranquil, restful bedroom. Used subtly, plants can enhance the mood, though it is probably unwise to use too many large leafy specimens (unless you long to sleep in a jungle!). Whites and pale blues are restful colours, and a simple white orchid always works well however the room is styled. Guest bedrooms, in particular, should be made welcoming; guests will feel very special indeed if their room is furnished with a beautiful flowering plant placed there especially for their stay.

Home office

If you work from home or manage the family affairs in a home office, then a fresh-air plant is a real advantage (see page 101). Not only will it provide a welcome slice of the natural world amongst all the inevitable hi-tech gadgets, it will actually make the atmosphere more pleasant to work in.

LEFT *A Boston fern is one of the best plants for creating 'fresh air', so it makes an excellent choice for perking up a workstation while creating a more pleasant atmosphere in which to work. The little Bird's Nest fern also adds a healthy note to the home office.*

RIGHT *This wonderful display of pink flowering plants will convince any guest they are incredibly welcome.*

Dining room

As well as the permanent plants used to decorate this room, you can use smaller seasonal flowering plants placed at the centre of the table to add a splash of colour. Or choose plants to suit the theme of the meal to add a touch of theatre to the dining table for a special occasion. When using plants to dress the table keep them small so they do not occupy too much valuable table space and so that diners can talk easily over them. At long tables, three or five small pots placed at intervals down the table will be more appropriate and perhaps more effective than one display at the centre of the table.

Conservatory

Traditionally, the conservatory was a room or building dedicated to plants, the home of precious plant collections. Now conservatories are more likely to be the result of a desire for additional living space. A conservatory often functions as a sitting room, dining room, playroom or even home office first, and plants are seen as an afterthought. A traditional conservatory would have been equipped for the convenience of the plant and gardener with potting benches, hard floors and drains, whereas now the emphasis is on the comfort of the human occupants rather than plants. So when placing plants in a conservatory the same concerns about watering, humidity and light to keep them healthy apply as they would in the rest of the house.

The conservatory's big advantage is light, masses of it. However, the glass construction alone does not guarantee a universally hospitable environment, suitable for all plants. Regulating the ventilation and shading in the room is vital in order to provide good growing conditions. The sun coming directly through the glass will scorch the foliage of many plants; equally, winter temperatures in an unheated conservatory will kill many exotic plants that one would normally expect to thrive in the conservatory. Higher temperatures mean the plants will need higher humidity.

TOP AND ABOVE *This conservatory is used as an informal dining room but it is still home to a wide range of plants. A large pepper plant (above) sits happily on a stool catching the maximum amount of light.*

FAR LEFT *A series of pretty cyclamen popped into simple teacups along the centre of the dining room table add a decorative note without occupying too much valuable table space.*

So before cramming your conservatory with fantastic specimen plants, consider the conditions, in winter and summer, just as you would in any other room and buy plants accordingly. If you intend to keep the conservatory frost-free, it can be a great place to over-winter specimens that are too tender to remain outside. Very hot conditions will suit cacti and succulents as well as floriferous plumbago and bougainvillea. In the right conditions, climbers can be given free rein to smother walls, and grape vines, jasmines and Passion flowers will all do well in the protected conditions. Of the palms, the miniature Date palm and the Ponytail palm are good choices for a hot conservatory. You might even consider growing some fruit and vegetables in ornamental containers.

Plant care basics

Caring for most houseplants is fairly straightforward as their requirements are simple: water, food and light. There is very little you need in the way of specialist equipment to care for houseplants; you do not have to become an 'indoor gardener' nor do you require green fingers, just a bit of common sense and basic information. For the most part, a plant will require a few seconds of your time each week when watering, less than that in the winter and the most arduous task is potting on every few years for long-term plants.

There are problems that may be encountered but in general 'killing' a plant is down to one of three problems: under- or over-watering; buying a plant in bad health; and expecting a plant that has been grown (and sold) as a for-the-moment plant to last forever. Within this chapter you will find advice on how to combat common and less common problems, as well as plant care profiles for many of the common houseplants featured in this book.

Choosing a good plant

TOOLS

There are nifty kits of tiny tools for the indoor gardener, however, most of us will never need them; scissors or garden secateurs and small watering can with a long spout are about all that is required, along with some soft twine for climbers perhaps.

This really requires a two-pronged approach – one for seasonal plants and one for more permanent plants. When purchasing seasonal plants all you need to take into consideration are good looks and the absence of pests that might infect other plants in the house. The bigger the better is a rule of thumb for these plants, and buy flowering plants in bud rather than in bloom in order to get the maximum flowering time out of your plant. Check that careless watering has not damaged the foliage and buds. Take a plant out of the display and check its shape since being crammed onto a bench makes for a good display but can adversely affect the shape of the individual plant.

For plants you hope to nurture long term, it pays to take a little more care, particularly if you are investing in a large specimen. It helps to go out with a good idea of what type of plant will thrive in the spot you have to fill and to find a supplier who you feel has provided the plant with a good standard of care. For the most part, plants will have already moved from grower to retailer, possibly through a middleman, probably travelling hundreds of kilometres before spending days or weeks on the benches of the retailer. Plants that have been well cared for during all of these transitions are most likely to thrive.

Look for a healthy plant: reject any with damaged leaves, browning foliage, holes in the leaves or any other signs of pests or disease. Plants need to look well, vibrant with some new growth, but not too much. The largest plant is not always the best – 'leggy' plants may have been kept in low light levels and growth that is more compact can give a better-looking plant. The surface of the compost should be clean and in most cases, roots should not be growing out of the base or the top of the pot (palms and orchids are the exceptions to the rule here).

Watering and feeding

Watering is the most troublesome aspect of growing indoor plants; it can be hard to get right since plants require different amounts of water delivered in a number of ways. Too much water is as likely to kill a plant as too little. In fact, under-watering is easier to deal with than over-watering since a dry plant wilts, the equivalent of a loud unmistakeable scream for water. An over-watered plant will look generally unwell and its foliage will turn yellow, symptoms that are easily confused with disease or even under-feeding.

ABOVE *Misting those plants that love humidity will pay dividends – your plants will look better and thrive.*

Watering routinely is not possible. Each plant has its own preference as to how dry its compost becomes before it is watered. The rate at which the compost dries out will depend on temperature and humidity, factors that will vary from season to season and from room to room. However, walking around once a week (twice a week for plants in small pots) with the watering can and assessing what actually needs watering and how much, should work. Regardless of many plants you have, fixing this chore in time helps. There is no shortcut to knowing how damp each plant likes its compost, and just looking will not do; you need to poke your finger gently into the compost at the edge of the pot. During the dormant period in winter, most plants require less frequent watering.

It is also important to know how each plant likes to be watered, most plants are watered directly onto the compost; African violets should be watered into a saucer to protect their leaves, some bromeliads have a funnel of leaves that should be filled with water, while Air plants are happy being swished in a bowl of water. Many plants prefer rainwater, especially the ericaceous, lime-hating azaleas and gardenias. Leave very cold water to reach room temperature before watering. Refer to the specific plant profile for watering information (see pages 132–41).

Dealing with wilting

If a plant does dry out and wilt, all is not lost. Most plants will recover miraculously from quite severe wilting, so never discard a wilted plant until you have tried to revive it. The problem is getting the water into the compost if it has dried out completely; the solution is to submerge the whole pot in a sink or bowl of water and leave the water to permeate the compost. Some growing mediums become so light when they dry out that the potted plant may float, in which case you need to hold the pot under until it takes on sufficient water to become stable.

Holiday watering

There are a number of strategies to get your plants through a period of absence, the most straightforward of which is to get a green-fingered friend to look after them. Otherwise, the best solution is to move plants temporarily to a reasonably cool room and use capillary wicks tucked well into the compost of each plant, the other end being dipped in large vessel of water. In this way moisture lost from each pot can be replaced as water travels up the wicks into the compost. It is even possible to fashion your own wicks from strips of old towel rather than buying them. I recommend you set up the system a day or two before departure to ensure it works.

Another way to set things up is to stand plants on a large tray or in the bath on a layer of capillary matting – again an old towel may suffice. In reality, if you have reasonably sized plants, they should survive a week or two without watering in a cool spot, especially if they are given a good soaking before you go. If you are away a great deal, choose plants from the list below.

BELOW *Holiday watering is no problem with this Umbrella sedge; before you leave, simply stand the whole pot in a larger container filled with water.*

Plants for those who can't get it right

If you want glorious houseplants to embellish your home but just cannot seem to nail watering them properly, or are away from home so much that watering is patchy, then there are a few plants that may suit you. Although these plants will carry on through spells of drought, some will survive longer than others and no plant, regardless of how tough it is, can live indefinitely without water.

SUCCULENTS AND DESERT CACTI: These plants have evolved to cope with very little water, so they should survive infrequent watering. They will definitely not tolerate over-watering.

PAPYRUS: This magnificent aquatic plant will look after itself if stood in a large receptacle of water. Use a generous-sized vessel and you will only have to top it up every few months.

CARNIVOROUS PLANTS: These unconventionally beautiful if slightly macabre group of plants are natives of acid bogs, so as long as they sit in a vessel of water they will grow well but only use rainwater.

AIR PLANTS: These do need dipping in water once or twice a week but it is incredibly easy; swish them in the water, shake them off and that is it – no scope for over-watering (see pages 90–91).

PONYTAIL PALM: I love this plant; it is good-looking, exotic and tolerant. As it stores water in its bulbous trunk, this palm will survive periods of drought.

MOTHER-IN-LAW's TONGUE: A remarkably tough plant, it will survive long periods without water, though will prosper when given water regularly.

ASPIDISTRA: Another survivor, with just a modicum of TLC it will flourish, but it will withstand lack of water.

SILVER DOLLAR PLANT: The fleshy leaves of *Crassula arborescens* store plenty of water so it will tolerate periods of drought and erratic watering.

WEEPING FIG: If you are reasonably reliable at watering, this pretty plant is worth a try. Though it may lose some leaves, it will revive after periods without enough water.

Feeding your plants

A remarkable number of people simply omit to feed their houseplants and then are surprised when they fail to thrive. Houseplants are growing in a small amount of compost, so the nutrition held in the growing medium soon becomes depleted and is washed away by watering. This makes it especially important to provide each plant with adequate fertilizer. There are specialist plant foods tailored to the needs of particular plant groups, citrus or orchids for example, but for most houseplants an all-purpose fertilizer will do. Liquid foods, mixed in the watering can to the manufacturer's specifications, are delivered when the plant is watered, and are easily drawn up by the plant. The need to apply food regularly to hungry plants in the growing season is rather a chore. For the time-poor or forgetful, slow-release spikes or pellets make the job much easier; pushed into the soil they release nutrients into the soil gradually and some last for an entire growing season.

A lack of nutrition will produce a sickly-looking plant; it will be more prone to attack from pests and diseases and will produce little or no new growth. Revive a hungry plant with liquid feed that it can draw up quickly, but do not be tempted to over-feed. This can be just as damaging, producing a miserable plant with scorched leaves. Some plants need feeding more frequently than others (see specific plant profiles on pages 132–141).

TOP *The lime-green trumpets of this elegant Pitcher Plant are designed to lure insects to their death; they tumble down the tube and are digested.*

ABOVE *A pellet of slow-release plant food is the simplest method of feeding plants through the growing season.*

Humidity and dust

Many plants prefer a more humid atmosphere than most of us have in our houses, because we use central heating and air conditioning to make our living spaces comfortable for us. This means that for many plants, particularly those natives to tropical and sub-tropical regions, it is essential to create some extra humidity in the air immediately around them to keep foliage lush, particularly in high temperatures.

The easiest way to achieve this is to mist plants regularly. An inexpensive spray bottle will fire a fine mist of water droplets into the air around the plant, increasing the humidity. Allow the water in the spray bottle to reach room temperature, then give each plant a good blast of water droplets. Another method is to stand the plant in a pebble tray – this is a shallow dish filled with pebbles and water. The pebbles are there to prevent the plant actually sitting in the water, which may rot the roots.

Plants use their leaves to absorb radiant energy in the form of light, which they use in the process of photosynthesis to produce sugars, which are used for energy. Plants also expel waste products from their leaves. Both these processes require the surface of the leaves to be clear of dust – if leaves are covered in dust the plant just cannot 'work' properly. There are all kinds of wipes and leaf shines available to clean the surface of leaves, but these are not necessary; often trying to wipe the leaves with a damp cloth will create a slurry over the leaves, which is also not helpful. It is best to use a soft brush just to whisk the dust away if leaves get dusty.

Alternatively, swish small plants in a bowl of water to clean their leaves or place larger plants outside in a gentle shower of rain if it is warm enough.

ABOVE *Succulents such as this are fairly free from problems, pests and diseases. They also don't require huge amounts of water.*

Pests and diseases

Healthy plants should be able to withstand disease and shrug off a minor pest attack if you spot it quickly enough. While you water, do a quick check for signs of pests and disease. Dealing with any problem quickly is not just important to save the infected plant but the other plants in the house as well. Unfortunately, some pests will spread quickly to other suitable hosts. Use the information on the opposite page which lists a number of common pests and diseases that prey on houseplants.

ABOVE *Productive plants such as these peppers do well and look good in a conservatory; however, they can be more susceptible to some pests when raised indoors.*

Common pests

APHIDS: This group of insects includes blackfly; they all suck sap from the plant, weakening it, leaving a sticky residue behind. They often carry viruses from plant to plant. Spotted early enough, aphids can simply be wiped away – small plants can be turned upside down and swished in a bowl of water, while larger, robust ones can be moved outside and a jet of water from the hose used to dislodge the insects.

LEAF MINER: You will not see the leaf miner, just its work. They make tiny wiggling tunnels below the cuticle of the leaf, clearly visible through the surface of the leaf. A mild infestation should not be a problem to a healthy plant if you react quickly and snip off all affected leaves.

LEAF ROLLER: This larva stage of the *Tortrix* moth curls one or two leaves up to form a shelter and ventures out to feast on leaves and stems. Eradicate the larva by removing the curled leaves.

RED SPIDER MITE: A particular problem in warm conditions, this pest can cause stunted growth in a plant, yellowing leaves and leaf distortion. The tiny mites are yellowish green in summer, making them difficult to spot, but further evidence of their presence is a fine web on the underside of leaves. A spell outside if the conditions are right will not harm the plant, and should be enough to stop them.

SCALE INSECT: Feeding on the sap of the plant, scale insect will weaken a plant and cause it to wilt. The insects are stationary; you will just see tiny bumps on the stem of the plant. Wipe them away with a cotton ball soaked in soapy water.

WHITE FLY: These tiny flies have white wings and are usually found on the underside of leaves where they suck sap from the plant, weakening it and potentially spreading harmful viruses. They also excrete an unpleasant sticky honeydew that adheres to the leaves.

Diseases

BOTRYTIS: This is a grey fluffy mould that occurs on all kinds of plants, both indoors and outside. As soon as you spot it, cut off all the affected parts of the plant until you reach into healthy tissue and check your watering regime.

MILDEW: A fungal infection, evidenced by a white powder developing on leaves and stems. Cut away all affected growth into healthy tissue.

SOOTY MOULD: A black fungus that grows on the honeydew deposited by aphids. It spoils the appearance of plants and can hamper the proper functioning of the leaves. Fortunately, it can simply be wiped away.

Quick problem solver

Unfortunately, many problems result in similar symptoms in houseplants, but if you consider the possible causes of a problem and think about the care the plant has received, it is normally possible to work out the most likely culprit.

ABOVE *Spring bulbs like these Grape hyacinths are unlikely to be inside long enough to pose many problems beyond wilting through lack of water.*

Yellowing leaves
- Too much water (slow change)
- Chilled
- Shock, change in position
- Sudden change in temperature

Yellowing leaves that do not drop
- Too much lime in water (the solution is to use rainwater)

Brown crispy leaves
- Sunscorch
- Over-feeding

Brown tipped leaves
- Too little water
- Too little humidity

Wilting
- Lack of water (if the pot feels light, it will be lack of water)
- Over-feeding

Slow growth
- Lack of feeding
- Needs repotting
- Wrong situation
- Too little water

Flower buds drop
- Lack of water
- Lack of humidity
- Moving the plant

Tall and leggy
- Light levels too low
- Too little fertilizer

Pale, blistered foliage with brown patches
- Sunscorch

Drooping leaves
- Too cold
- Too draughty
- Over-feeding
- Too much direct sunlight

Failing to flower
- Too little light/dark
- Wrong temperature
- Too little fertilizer

Potting on

The need to move a young plant from one pot to another that is slightly larger will vary between types of plants. Move plants to a pot only a bit larger than the one it is currently in; giving a plant plenty of space all at once can cause problems. Once plants get to a certain size and maturity, potting on becomes impossible, so in this situation remove the top 5–7.5 cm (2–3 in) of compost and replaced with fresh compost. As a rule, even young plants will only need potting on every one or two years.

There are many specialized growing mediums tailored to meet the needs of a particular group of plants such as cacti and succulents, orchids, bonsai or citrus fruits. For most others the distinction is merely whether they would do best in a loam-based or loam-free compost. The plant profiles give an indication of which compost to choose (see pages 132–41). Though tempting it is not wise to use garden soil; it is unlikely to be the perfect growing medium for the plant and it may contain pests and viruses.

LEFT *Not all plants need potting on each year; some prefer to be a little pot-bound while others, like these Aeoniums, will tolerate living in the same pot for a number of years.*

Plant care profiles

Though there are usually specific instructions for feeding, in most cases using a slow-release plant food pellet or liquid is by far the easiest option. The minimum temperatures listed here serve as a guide for those who might wish to keep their plants in an unheated conservatory.

Aechmea

Bromeliads of various species

LIGHT Bright indirect light

WATER Put water in funnel; keep roots moist

FEED Weak liquid fertilizer into funnel in summer

TEMP Minimum 15°C (59°F)

Aeonium arboreum 'Schwarzkopf'

Aeonium

LIGHT Full sun

WATER Minimal water, almost none in winter

FEED Feed with cactus fertilizer

TEMP Minimum 10°C (50°F)

NOTES Needs well-drained compost

Alocasia amazonica

African Mask; Amazon Lily

LIGHT Partial shade

WATER Keep compost moist with warm water; mist frequently

FEED Every two weeks in summer

TEMP Minimum 18.5°C (65°F)

NOTES Poisonous; skin and eye irritant

Aloe vera

Aloe

LIGHT Full sun

WATER Allow compost to dry between watering; minimal water in winter

FEED Occasionally

TEMP Minimum 5°C (41°F)

Anigozanthos manglesii, A. flavidus

Kangaroo Paw, Cat's Paw

LIGHT Bright indirect light

WATER Generously with rainwater in the growing season, less in winter

FEED Monthly with azalea food in the summer

TEMP Minimum 10–12°C (50–54°F)

Aspidistra elatior

Cast-iron plant

LIGHT Bright indirect light to a really gloomy corner

WATER Keep compost moist in summer; water sparsely in winter

FEED Once a month in the growing season

TEMP Minimum 7–10°C (45–50°F)

NOTES Only killed by over-watering or incredibly dim light

Asplenium nidus

Bird's Nest fern

LIGHT Indirect light to shade

WATER Keep compost moist; mist regularly

FEED Monthly with weak plant food

TEMP Minimum 15.5°C (60°F)

NOTES Enjoys bottom heat

Asplenium scolopendrium

Hart's Tongue fern

LIGHT Partial shade

WATER Keep compost moist at all times; though less so in winter

FEED Liquid feed once a month in spring and summer

TEMP Minimum -5°C (23°F)

NOTES Usually planted outside, it makes a tolerant houseplant

Asplenium nidus

Azalea indica

Azalea, Indian Azalea

LIGHT Bright indirect light to partial shade

WATER Freely with soft water; mist leaves regularly

FEED Azalea food weekly in growing season

TEMP Ideal 10–15.5°C (50–60°F)

NOTES Prefers a cool room

Begonia rex

Begonia

LIGHT Bright indirect light

WATER Freely in growing season, less in winter; likes good humidity but not misting so use a pebble tray

FEED Regularly in the growing season

TEMP Fine in average room tempertures 21–24°C (70–75°F); minimum temperature 16°C (61°F)

NOTES Repot annually in spring; poisonous

Crocus

Bougainvillea glabra

Bougainvillea

LIGHT Sun or bright indirect light; good in a conservatory

WATER Keep compost moist in summer, water less in winter and allow to almost dry

FEED Weekly in summer

TEMP Minimum 7–10°C (45–50°F); too much heat reduces flowering

NOTES Prune as required in spring

Calathea zebrina

Calathea, Zebra plant

LIGHT Bright indirect light to partial shade

WATER Likes plenty of water and high humidity so mist leaves and use a pebble tray

FEED Bi-weekly

TEMP Minimum 15°C (59°F)

Chamaedorea elegans

Parlour palm

LIGHT Bright indirect light to partial shade

WATER Generously through the growing season; spray leaves occasionally, especially in warm temperature eratures

FEED With dilute plant food every two weeks

TEMP Average room temperature 16°C (61°F)

Chlorophytum comosum

Spider plant

LIGHT Bright to partially shaded position

WATER Keep compost moist in summer, water less frequently in winter; mist occasionally

FEED Every two weeks in summer

TEMP Minimum 7°C (45°F)

NOTES May enjoy summer outdoors in a sheltered spot if the weather is good

Cissus rhombifolia

Grape ivy, Oak-leaf ivy

LIGHT Indirect light to partial shade

WATER Keep the compost moist all year round, water slightly less in the winter

FEED Weekly in the summer

TEMP Ideal for a cool to warm room; minimum temperature 13°C (55°F)

NOTES Allow to trail or provide trellis or moss pole

Clivia miniata

Bush Lily, Clivia

LIGHT Good light, no direct sun. Light, cool in the winter; move to warmer spot once buds form

WATER Keep the compost just moist in the summer and drier in winter

FEED Every two weeks from spring to late summer

TEMP Cool to normal room; must be cool in winter to bloom: 4.5–10°C (40–50°F) is ideal

NOTES Toxic

Crassula ovata

Jade tree, Money plant

LIGHT Full sun to bright position

WATER Very little in the summer and less in the winter

FEED Once a month

TEMP Minimum 15°C (59°F)

NOTES Enjoys summer outside

Crocus chrysanthus, C. vernus

Crocus

LIGHT Indirect bright light.

WATER Keep compost moist

FEED After blooming, feed when the bulbs are planted out in the garden

TEMP Minimum -8°C (18°F)

NOTES Plant bulbs in autumn to flower in early spring, in bulb fibre and leave in pots outside until buds form, then move pots inside to a cool room

Cryptanthus bivittatus

Earth Star

LIGHT Bright indirect light

WATER Keep compost barely moist, using soft water; mist frequently

FEED Very dilute fertilizer every two weeks

TEMP Warm temperatures, around 21°C (70°F), required to bring into flower; minimum 10°C (50°F)

Cycas revoluta

Sago palm

LIGHT Bright light, no direct sun

WATER Keep compost just moist through the growing season; mist in high temperatures

FEED Once every two weeks to once a month in the growing season

TEMP Will tolerate cool room to really hot spot; very tolerant. Minimum temperature 7°C (45°F)

NOTES Slow-growing; can spend the summer outside protected from rain

Cyclamen persicum

Cyclamen

LIGHT Indirect light

WATER Keep root ball just moist when in bloom (corms can rot)

FEED Once every two weeks when in bloom

TEMP Likes a cool room, maximum 15.5° (60°F)

Cymbidium hybrids

Boat orchids

LIGHT Bright light to partial shade

WATER Freely and mist frequently in the growing season

FEED With orchid food once a month

TEMP Minimum winter temperature 13°C (55°F)

NOTES Enjoys a cool, well-ventilated airy room (not draughty)

Cyperus involucratus

Umbrella sedge, Umbrella plant

LIGHT Bright light

WATER Freely at all times, plant can stand in water; mist regularly

FEED Feed in growing season

TEMP Minimum 7°C (45°F)

Cyperus papyrus

Papyrus Sedge, Egyptian Paper Rush

LIGHT Bright light, will tolerate some direct sun

WATER Place pot in a watertight container and stand pot in a few inches of water; mist foliage regularly

FEED In growing season

TEMP Ideally warm all year round but will tolerate low temperatures; minimum temperature 7°C (45°F)

Cyrtomium falcatum

Fishtail Fern, Japanese Holly Fern and *C. falcatum* 'Rochfordianum' (Holly Fern)

LIGHT Some shade to bright indirect light

WATER Freely in the growing season; mist regularly. Keep compost moist in winter

FEED Liquid fertilizer every two weeks through the summer

TEMP Minimum -5°C (23°F)

Cyperus papyrus

Dracaena marginata

Dragon Tree and *D. draco* (Madegascar Dragon Tree)

LIGHT Bright indirect light though will adapt to some direct light and partial shade

WATER Keep the compost just moist in summer, drier in winter; mist foliage regularly

FEED Every two weeks throughout the summer

TEMP Minimum 13°C (55.5°F)

Echeveria

(including *E. agavoides*, *E. glauca*, *E. elegans*, *E. dereubergii*)

LIGHT Sun to bright indirect light

WATER Sparingly; even less in winter, just enough to stop leaves from crinkling

FEED With cactus food once or twice in the growing season

TEMP Minimum 10°C (50°F)

Erica

Echinocactus grusonii

Barrel Cactus, Mother-in-law's
Cushion

LIGHT Full light

WATER Freely in the summer but
do not waterlog the compost; leave
to dry between waters in winter.

FEED Once a month with half-
strength fertilizer

TEMP Minimum 10°C (50°F)

Epipremnum aureum

Pothos, Devil's Ivy

LIGHT Bright indirect light

WATER Keep compost moist during
the growing season, drier in winter

FEED Every two weeks in spring
and summer

TEMP Minimum 18°C (65°F)

NOTES Poisonous; skin and eye
irritant

Erica

Heathers

LIGHT Bright light to partial shade

WATER With soft water so compost
is just moist

FEED Every two weeks with a
fertilizer designed for ericaceous
plants

TEMP Will do best in a cool room.
Minimum below -12°C (10°F)

NOTES These are just temporary
visitors indoors but can remain in
for a couple of weeks or so. Return
to the garden once flowering has
finished

Euphorbia pulcherrima

Poinsettia

LIGHT Bright indirect light

WATER Sparingly so compost is
barely moist while flowering; mist
occasionally

FEED Through the summer until
the plant is in flower

TEMP Minimum 13°C (55°F) when
in flower

NOTES Keep in darkness for 14
hours a day from mid-autumn for
eight weeks to trigger flowering. Sap
is skin irritant

Fatsia japonica

Japanese Aralia, Castor Oil Plant

LIGHT Good light to shade

WATER Keep just moist in summer
and prevent compost from drying
out in winter

FEED Once a month when the plant
is in growth

TEMP Tolerates cool temperature
and draughts; not suited to very
warm rooms; minimum -5°C (23°F)

Ficus benjamina

Weeping Fig

LIGHT Bright indirect light

WATER Keep compost just moist
though it will survive being allowed
to dry out

FEED In spring and summer

TEMP Minimum 13°C (55°F)

NOTES May cause allergic skin
reactions

Ficus elastica

Rubber plant; India Rubber Fig

LIGHT Bright light, no direct sun

WATER Keep root ball moist

FEED Once a month in the summer

TEMP Minimum 13°C (55°F)

NOTES A tough plant but dislikes
being moved once settled; prune
central stem to create a bushy
plant; toxic

Ficus pumila

Creeping Fig; Climbing Fig

LIGHT Partial shade

WATER Keep compost moist; mist
leaves regularly

FEED Monthly in spring and
summer

TEMP Minimum 7°C (45°F)

Fittonia

Nerve Plant, Mosaic Plant

LIGHT Partial shade

WATER Freely in spring and summer,
less frequently in winter; mist
regularly and use a pebble tray

FEED With a weak fertilizer every
few weeks

TEMP Minimum 15.5°C (60°F)

Gardenia jasminoides

Gardenia

LIGHT Good bright light but no direct sun

WATER Keep compost moist in spring and summer and a little drier in winter; mist plant regularly

FEED With non-alkaline azalea fertilizer

TEMP Requires a fairly constant temperature of around 19.5°C (67°F)

Gerbera

African Daisy, Transvaal Daisy

LIGHT Full sun to bright light

WATER Keep compost moist while plant is growing and a little drier in the winter; mist leaves regularly

FEED Every two weeks during the growing season

TEMP Needs temperatures of 13–21ºC (55–70ºF) to do well; minimum temperature 5ºC (41ºF)

Gloriosa superba 'Rothschildiana'

Flame Lily, Glory Lily

LIGHT Sun or bright light

WATER Freely

FEED Feed once a week in summer

TEMP Keep tubers in pot at 13°C (50ºF); start water in spring and sprout tubers at 20°C (68°F)

NOTES Poisonous

Guzmania

(including *G. lingulata* and *Guzmania* hybrids)

LIGHT Indirect, bright light

WATER Freely through the growing season; mist regularly

FEED With dilute fertilizer every few weeks

TEMP Minimum 15.5°C (60°F)

Haworthia

(including *H. margaritifera, H. fasciata, H. tessellata*)

LIGHT Full sun, bright light

WATER Sparingly; less in the winter

FEED Cactus food once a month

TEMP Minimum 13°C (55°F)

Hedera helix

Common Ivy

LIGHT Indirect light but will tolerate poor light

WATER Keep roots moist

FEED Every two weeks or so in the growing season

TEMP Prefers a cool room; hardy to -15ºC (5°F)

NOTES Poisonous; skin irritant

Helleborus

Hellebores

LIGHT Bright indirect light to partial shade

WATER Keep the root ball moist

TEMP Prefers a cool room; will survive temperature to -15ºC (5°F)

NOTES Return to the garden once flowering has finished

Helleborus

Hippeastrum

Amaryllis

LIGHT Bright light

WATER Keep compost moist

FEED After flowering until growth wilts

TEMP Minimum 18.5°C (65°F)

NOTES Toxic

Howea forsteriana

Kentia Palm

LIGHT Indirect light to partial shade; tolerates shade

WATER Let the compost dry out slightly before you water, keep compost just moist in winter; mist foliage regularly, especially when it is warm

FEED With palm fertilizer throughout the summer

TEMP Minimum 10ºC (50°F)

Hydrangea

Hyacinthus

Hyacinth

LIGHT Bright indirect light; flowers fade more quickly in warm rooms

WATER Keep compost moist

FEED Once flowers fade, feed with liquid fertizer and plant out in the garden after risk of frost has gone

TEMP Blooms last longer in a cool spot. Minimum -8°C (18°F)

NOTES Plant in autmn for winter blooms, later for later flowering. Plant in bulb fibre. Leave pot in dark cool spot until shoots are 5 cm (2 in) high, then bring into a cool room until they are ready to display

Hydrangea x macrophylla

Common Hydrangea

LIGHT Indirect light

WATER Keep compost moist

TEMP Cool room; minimum temperature -15°C (5°F)

NOTES Plant out in the garden once flowering has finished

Kalanchoe blossfeldiana

Flaming Katy

LIGHT Bright indirect light, tolerates some direct sun

WATER Keep compost just moist during growing season, drier in the winter

FEED Liquid fertilizer every two weeks during growing season

TEMP Minimum 10°C (50°F)

NOTES Toxic

Kalanchoe 'Magic Bells'

Kalanchoe Magic Bells

LIGHT Bright light, some direct sun

WATER Keep compost moist while the plant is growing but drier in the winter

FEED Every two weeks during growing season

TEMP Minimum 10°C (50°F)

NOTES Toxic

Lavandula

Lavender

LIGHT Bright indirect light; this is only a temporary visitor from the garden

WATER Keep the compost just moist

TEMP Blooms last longer in a cool spot. Minimum -8°C (18°F)

NOTES Cut back and return to the garden once flowering is over

Monstera deliciosa

Swiss Cheese plant

LIGHT Good indirect light to shade

WATER Keep compost moist during growing season, water sparingly in winter; mist leaves regularly

FEED With liquid fertilizer once a month during growing season

TEMP Keep at normal room temperature; minimum temperature 10°C (50°F)

NOTES Poisonous, eye and skin irritant; provide climbing support

Muscari armeniacum

Grape Hyacinth

LIGHT Sun to partial shade; keep pot outside until the bulbs produce leaves and flower shoots

WATER Keep roots moist

FEED Give a liquid feed after flowering and before planting out in the garden

TEMP Ideal is about 18°C (65°F) when flowering. The flowers last longer in cool rooms

NOTES Toxic; can be returned to the garden once it has finished flowering

Narcissus

Daffodil, Narcissus

LIGHT Bright indirect light; flowers fade more quickly in a warm room

WATER Keep compost moist

FEED Once flowers fade, feed with liquid fertizer and plant out in the garden after risk of frost has gone

TEMP Blooms last longer in a cool spot. Minimum -8°C (18°F)

NOTES Plant in autumn for spring flowering. Plant in bulb fibre and leave pot in dark cool spot until shoots are 5 cm (2 in) high, then bring into a cool room until they are ready to display. Toxic.

Neoregelia carolinae

Blushing Bromeliad

LIGHT Good bright light, no direct sun

WATER Wet compost moderately using only soft water; mist regularly

FEED With a weak fertilizer every two weeks during growing season

TEMP Minimum 13ºC (55ºF)

Nephrolepis exaltata 'Bostoniensis'

Boston Fern

LIGHT Bright indirect light to shade

WATER Freely, do not allow compost to dry out; spray regularly and sit in pebble tray

FEED Monthly with dilute fertilizer in summer

TEMP Minimum 7–10ºC (45–50ºF)

Oncidium hybrids

Tiger orchids

LIGHT Bright indirect light to partial shade

WATER Moderately in summer, ensure all residual water drains out between waters; mist regularly

FEED With orchid food every two weeks during growing season

TEMP 15.5–29.5ºC (60–85ºF)

Peperomia caperata

Emerald Ripple (and *P. argyreia* – Watermelon Peperomia)

LIGHT Good indirect light to partial shade

WATER Moderately in summer; mist leaves occasionally during summer

FEED Half-strength liquid fertilizer every two weeks in spring and summer

TEMP Minimum 15ºC (59ºF)

Phalaenopsis hybrids

Moth orchids

LIGHT Good indirect light to partial shade

WATER Keep growing medium just moist all year; mist regularly

FEED With orchid food every two weeks during spring and summer

TEMP Minimum 13ºC (55ºF)

Philodendron scandens

Sweetheart plant

LIGHT Light shade or indirect light

WATER Well in summer; just damp in winter; mist regularly

FEED A liquid feed once a month or so in spring and summer

TEMP Average room temperature. Minimum winter temperature 13ºC (55ºF)

NOTES Poisonous; eye and skin irritant

Phoenix roebelenii

Pygmy Date Palm; Miniature Date Palm

LIGHT Good light, some direct sun

WATER Moderately during growing season, sparingly in winter

FEED Regularly during the growing season

TEMP Minimum 15.5ºC (60ºF)

NOTES Toxic

Pilea cadierei

Aluminium Plant

LIGHT Good indirect light to partial shade

WATER Moderately during growing season; mist leaves regularly

FEED Half-strength liquid fertilizer every two weeks in spring and summer

TEMP 13ºC (55ºF)

Plumbago

Plumbago, Leadwort

LIGHT Direct sunlight

WATER Generously in summer, keep soil moist in winter

FEED High potash fertilizer every two weeks in spring and summer

TEMP Minimum 7–10ºC (45–50ºF) in winter

NOTES Toxic

Primula acaulis

Primrose (also *P. vulgaris*, *P. obconica* – Poison Primrose)

LIGHT Bright indirect light, some direct sun

WATER Moderately in spring and summer, sparingly in winter; mist leaves occasionally

FEED With general liquid fertilizer

TEMP Prefers a cool spot; minimum temperature 13ºC (55ºF)

NOTES Plant in the garden after flowering. *P. obconica* can be kept in a cool spot indoors and may flower again next year. It is also a skin irritant

Rhapis excelsa

Lady Palm

LIGHT Direct sun

WATER Moderately in spring and summer, sparingly in winter

FEED Every two weeks during the growing season

TEMP Normal room temperature but will adapt to a wide range; ideal minimum winter temperature 10°C (50°F)

Rosa

Rose

LIGHT Bright light

WATER Regularly, keep compost drier in winter

FEED Every two weeks in spring and summer

TEMP Minimum 7°C (45°F)

Saintpaulia

Africa Violet

LIGHT Good indirect light

WATER Keep compost moist during growing season, drier in winter

FEED Specialized fertilizer every two weeks in spring and summer

TEMP Dislikes extreme changes in temperature. Minimum temperature 15.5°C (60°F)

NOTES Likes good humidity but not misting so use a pebble tray

Sansevieria

Mother-in-law's Tongue

LIGHT Direct sun to partial shade

WATER Allow compost to dry slightly before watering in spring and summer, water sparingly in winter

FEED Half-strength liquid fertilizer once a month in summer

TEMP Minimum 10°C (50°F)

Sarracenia

Pitcher plant

LIGHT Good indirect light, tolerates some direct sun

WATER Generously with soft water, keep soil waterlogged; mist the leaves regularly

FEED For immature plants use liquid plant food at half-strength if insect populations are low

TEMP Prefers cooler spot in winter and can spend summer outside. Minimum temperature 5°C (41°F)

Schlumbergera

Christmas Cactus

LIGHT Indirect bright light

WATER Moderately in summer, reduce for 4 weeks to spark flowering; reduce water after flowering

FEED High potash fertilizer in summer

TEMP Minimum 10°C (50°F)

NOTES Can spend the summer outside

Solanum capsicastrum, S. pseudocapsicum

Winter Cherry

LIGHT Good indirect light, some direct sun

WATER Generously during growing period; mist leaves regularly

FEED Regularly in summer

TEMP Prefers a cool room. Minimum temperature 10°C (50°F)

NOTES Toxic

Soleirolia soleirolii

Baby's Tears, Mind-your-own-business

LIGHT Good indirect light

WATER Keep compost moist at all times; mist leaves regularly

FEED Half-strength liquid fertilizer every two weeks in spring and summer

TEMP Minimum -15°C (5°F)

Spathiphyllum wallisii

Peace Lily, Spathe Flower

LIGHT Good indirect light to partial shade

WATER Moderately during growing season, sparingly in winter; mist leaves regularly

FEED Every two weeks in spring and summer

TEMP Minimum 15.5°C (60°F)

NOTES Poisonous; skin and eye irritant

Stephanotis floribunda

Madagascar Jasmine

LIGHT Good indirect light, tolerates some direct sun

WATER Moderately during growing season, sparingly in winter; mist occasionally

FEED Every two weeks in summer

TEMP Minimum temperatures 18–21ºC (65–70ºF) in summer, 13–15.5ºC (55–60ºF) in winter

Syngonium

Arrowhead Vine, Goosefoot Vine

LIGHT Good indirect light to partial shade

WATER Moderately during growing season, sparingly in winter; mist leaves regularly

FEED Every two weeks in spring and summer

TEMP Minimum winter temperature 15.5ºC (60ºF)

NOTES Skin and eye irritant

Tradescantia

Inch Plant, Spiderwort (also *T. fluminensis, T. blossfeldiana, T. zebrina*)

LIGHT Good indirect light, some direct sun

WATER Moderately in spring and summer, sparingly in winter; mist occasionally

FEED Every two weeks in spring and summer

TEMP Minimum 7°C (45°F)

Tulipa

Tulip

LIGHT Direct sun to partial shade

WATER Keep soil moderately moist

FEED Once or twice between sprouting and flowering

TEMP Force or keep pots outside until buds form. Hardy, keep in cool conditions, ideal temperature 15.5–18°C (60–65°F)

NOTES Skin irritant; Can plant in garden once flowering is over

Viola tricolor, V. hybrida

Pansy, Viola

LIGHT Direct sun to partial shade

WATER Keep soil moderately moist

FEED As their stay inside will be short, feeding may not be necessary, but a dilute liquid feed may prolong flowering

TEMP Cool temperature

NOTES Plant in the garden once flowering is over

Vriesea splendens

Flaming Sword

LIGHT Direct sun to partial shade

WATER Moderately during growing season, sparingly in winter; mist leaves regularly in summer

FEED Weak fertilizer once a month in summer

TEMP Prefers a warm room. Minimum 15°C (59°F)

Tulipa

Yucca elephantipes, Y. aloifolia

Yuccas

LIGHT Good indirect light, some direct sun, will tolerate poor light

WATER Moderately during growing season, sparingly in winter

FEED Every two weeks in spring and summer

TEMP Minimum 7°C (45°F)

Zantedeschia aethiopica

Calla Lily and hybrids

LIGHT Direct sun to good light

WATER Keep compost moist, and keep wet when in flower

FEED Every two weeks during the flowering season

TEMP Cool to normal room temperatures; Calla Lily minimum -5°C (23°F), hybrids minimum 10°C (50°F)

NOTES Poisonous; skin and eye irritant

Index   <small>Page numbers in *italic* refer to illustrations</small>

Acknowledgements

My thanks to: Clive Nichols for his ravishing photography; Emma Bastow at New Holland for commissioning this project, which has been such a pleasure and Marilyn Inglis at New Holland for her skilful and determined editing, which has made this a better book; and also to Geoff Borin for his inspired design. Thanks also to House of Plants for arranging a speedy delivery of beautiful plants at the eleventh hour and to Nancy and Harriet for helping out. Finally, though the vast majority of the images in the book were shot in my homes, I would like to thank the others whose wonderful houseplants feature in the book.

My thanks to my family – David, Harriet, Nancy and Joshua – for cheerfully carrying on as photographic shoots go on around them and for tolerating my long hours spent hauled up with my laptop.